M000301850

"You will be challenged, inspired, and empowered after reading Dr. Jenn Dean-Hill's maiden book *Reclaiming Eden*. It is timely, it is relevant, and it is vital reading for women and men of all ages. Even though the world is in the midst of uncertainty and fear, *Reclaiming Eden* takes you on a journey of certainty—the exploration of biblical truths regarding gender equality. As a Social Work Clinician, Professor, and Christian leader, Dr. Dean-Hill's brilliant writing gives me radical hope of a more certain future—that of 'equity, unity, and love between the genders.'"

—*Dr. Jean Ollis, LISW-S, MSW, DMin*
Mental Health Therapist/Assistant Professor of Social Work

"In *Reclaiming Eden*, Dr. Jennifer Dean-Hill asks a thought-provoking question: 'What kind of marriage did Adam and Eve experience in the early garden days, and what church would they want to attend?' The story she tells and the principles she gives lead us into a deeper understanding of marriage, the church, and God's desire and plan for harmony and unity in both."

—*Dr. Jim Sabella, DMin*
Missionary Leader, Assemblies of God World Missions,
Europe Region

"We have become a people who outsource our faith to man-made social constructs that guide our perceptions and behaviors as they relate to love, marriage, partnership and connections of all kinds. We are not called to outsource our faith to these institutions. Jenn reminds us that God is IN all of us. We need to be open to his presence and listen to his calling. There is no hierarchy or subordination in the Trinity. God, Jesus, and the Holy Spirit do not compare, subordinate, and compete, they connect fully and offer self-giving love equally. Our most enriching connections are a reflection of the Trinity. We are joint heirs being called to complement, strengthen, and complete each other in life, at work, and at large."

—Dr. Jackie Freiberg and Dr. Kevin Freiberg
International Bestselling Authors, EpicWorkEpicLife

"*Reclaiming Eden* is the book I've been searching for. First, I am impressed by the comprehensive nature of this book. Dr. Jennifer Dean-Hill's analysis of the contemporary leadership issue in our society, specifically within the church, lays the framework for an exciting positive change. This book enables us to understand how we got where we are, but she doesn't leave us there. Second, I am pleased by the accessibility of this book, as Dr. Dean-Hill lays out steps any church can use toward incorporating Godly, gifted women into appropriate leadership positions within the local church. Her skills as a Social Worker are evident in *Reclaiming Eden*, which contains a wealth of practical guidance into precisely how we come to '...negotiating conversations, learning new conflict resolution skills, developing friendliness, and engaging in vulnerable communication.' This book is a gift from Jennifer to the Body of Christ and will in a practical way lead local church leadership to reclaim Eden within their church body, which will invigorate the church towards optimal leadership with the entire army of God."

—Dr. Cynthia Preszler, DMin
Ordained Minister, Marriage and Family Therapist

"True mutuality and partnership is something we often long for in marriage, but we also often find we have brought things into our marriage that get in the way of that aspiration. Now with this book you can identify what hinders you as a couple, and how together to create the marriage you always wanted. Be inspired, be equipped, and discover the change you long for."

—Dr. Jason Swan Clark, PhD, DMin
Lead Mentor, Leadership and Global Perspectives,
Portland Seminary

"This is an important book for people who are searching for community in church but feel stymied because they feel thwarted by patriarchal values that do not match their own hopes for an egalitarian lifestyle. The author shows, through the use of a mixture of positive psychology, scripture, and research on marriage, that church communities can and do exist that support a marriage of peers and traditional Christian values. In support of marriages where each partner's dignity and purpose are equally valued, Jennifer Dean-Hill writes a book to show others in church communities how that can be accomplished."

—*Pepper Schwartz, PhD*
Professor of Sociology, University of Washington

"Jennifer brings a super charged message to the church, marriage and the working of both genders! This Biblical imperative is articulated with insight as Jenn brings years of experience in ministry and clinical practice. Thank you for this work Jenn; I eagerly wait and work with you to see Eden in relationships.

—*Kristy Newport, LMFT*
Licensed Marriage & Family Therapist, Lay minister

RECLAIMING
EDEN

RECLAIMING
EDEN

*Creating a Peer Community for
Couples and Churches*

Written by
DR. JENNIFER DEAN-HILL
DMin, MSW, LICSW

ILLUMIFY MEDIA GLOBAL
Littleton, Colorado

RECLAIMING
EDEN

Copyright © 2020 by Jennifer Dean-Hill

The views and opinions expressed in this book are those of the author and do not necessarily reflect the official policy or position of Illumify Media Global.

About the cover artist: While artist Sue Shehan is inspired by all of nature, it is the Colorado skies that captivate her most. Her desire is to capture the viewer's imagination, and to invite them into the vibrant world of pastels.

Published by
Illumify Media Global
www.IllumifyMedia.com
"Write. Publish. Market. SELL!"

Library of Congress Control Number: 2020906039

Paperback ISBN: 978-1-949021-70-7
eBook ISBN: 978-1-949021-71-4

Typeset by Art Innovations (http://artinnovations.in/)
Cover design by Debbie Lewis

Printed in the United States of America

*To the Eden Maker who designed perfect garden living
and continues to do so
To the Trinity Team, Jackie, Kevin, Paul, Cindie,
and Jake, my authentic community
To my mini-church, Jake, who has inspired rich character
development and oneness within me*

CONTENTS

Section 3
Complete | Eden Living

ACKNOWLEDGEMENTS

To the churches who taught me about what I really loved in community and what I really dislike in community, blessings to all of you and the leaders daring enough to lead you and brave enough to leave you so they can reclaim their Eden. All the pastors, members, and leaders hold a special place in my heart for attempting to resurrect a bit of Eden again and bring heaven to earth.

Thank you to all who supported me in pursuing my dreams. Illumify Publishing, Karen, Mike, Geoff and all the faces I've yet to see but so grateful they have worked so kindly and respectfully with me to make this dream a reality. Portland Seminary with George Fox University and their daring leaders who dreamt up a leadership academic program I couldn't wait to join and enjoyed experiencing. To the Trinity Team I dreamt up on a walk and who all helped to make a reality. Your encouragement, support, and belief in me was more than I even thought to ask for, yet you all provided the loving community I didn't even know I needed in order to reclaim my own Eden. Blessings to each of you, my fellow world-changers with God-sized dreams in all your fabulous, creative, daring work. You inspire greatness in me.

To my clients, who have bravely opened their hearts to me and allowed me the honor of walking closely beside you. I continue to be honored and humbled at the courage and resiliency each of you shows to choose to heal, love, forgive, trust, and be in community with others. The life lessons you have taught me are too many to name, but your faces and stories will be held in the most sacred part of my heart forever. To my family, Jake, McKenna, and Dawson, and my supportive extended family, who have taught me the most about learning to live in community and given me opportunity to practice developing my spiritual values and character virtues with grace and love. Thank you for your love, encouragement, and grace. I love each of you dearly and am so blessed to call you family. A special thanks to Dr. Cynthia Preszler and our three-hour Starbucks meetings to hammer out how to speak this message in love so we can inspire change. You are a real life Wonder Woman, rich in experiences, daring in quests, and humble in heart. Thank you for your friendship, support, and wisdom. It has carried me through many turbulent waters and landed me upright again time after time. To my dear friends, thank you for always believing in me and my ability to lead, write, and create. Thank you for your love throughout the years and decades. I am so grateful for each of you.

To the people in countries and cities I've traveled to in the last four years who opened up their hearts and resources to me so I could broaden my education in how to lead and live in community together. London, Dublin, Paris, Bangkok, Cape Town, Johannesburg, Zimbabwe, Hong Kong, Beijing, Venice, Rome, Athens, Mykonos, Cabo. . . and more to come. I have been hungry to meet you all and so grateful for the experiences I've had in each magnificent place and the beautiful leaders and citizens who inhabit you.

I am grateful for the rich experiences, shared wisdom, and real relationships that have played a part in developing my leadership story. It is my turn to bless and inspire others for your contributions in my life.

May this work bless you.

FOREWORD

A ny system of hierarchy, while initially easier to navigate than authentic relationships, ultimately shutters the uniqueness of all participants, inhibits creativity, stunts personal growth and development, and fundamentally destroys the mystery of what it means to be human.

I was the passenger in a car being driven by my friend Richard Rohr when he said the following: "This may sound crazy coming from an old celibate Franciscan priest, but my years of experience have convinced me that one of the greatest gifts God ever gave the human race is marriage. And here is why: marriage forces us to stay in proximity to another human being long enough where our propensity to hide is potentially diminished and we are invited by sheer presence to do the work of transformation."

Matrix (Urban Dictionary): "A computer-generated dream world built to keep us under control in order to change a human being into a battery."

I confess I am one of those "religious folk" who grew up reading the Scriptures more to resolve my internal guilty-conscience regulator than to learn or hear anything. For some of us, years of absence from the legalism of "quiet time" allowed our give-a-damns time to heal and awaken desires for exploration that emerged from the inside. Interactions with voices of intelligent kindness and compelling authenticity outside our own experience and traditions blew fresh breath into the smoke of our confusion and disdain, initially fanning embers of careful curiosity into Cheshire-grin acknowledgement that we had missed something "good."

Turns out we are in a relationship with a God who by nature submits, and somewhere near the center of God's relentless affection for you and me is submission to our brokenness that God encounters in our hearts, souls, and minds. This is not self-less submission, but self-giving and other-centered. It is respectful of both the wonder of this high-order creation that is a human being and of its capacity for self-deception and lie-enshrouded power to devastate.

Ask any parent who has even a modicum of health about their love for their child, and you will be told that this love is unconditional, dependent on, and originating in the one loving. However, relationship, the mystery of how this love is expressed, is not unconditional, nor would we ever want it to be. It is one thing that *you* love me, another altogether that you *see* me. When a person dies, while it may not affect your love for them, I guarantee it will affect your relationship with them. By its very nature a real relationship creates a space of interaction in which knowing the "other" and their choices, character, and circumstance actually matters. It is a desperately beautiful sorrow that relationship means the other can say "no" or believe a lie, or be involved in accidents, or struggle with illness or addiction, or kiss you, or refuse to talk, or hide secrets, or leave you a note, or express kindness, or forgive or put up and take down walls.

But we human beings generally are a fearful lot, embedding our drive for certainty in expressions of power rather than in the risk of trust and relationship. We create (dream up) institutional systems and organizations of hierarchical power, be they religious, social, ideological, political, educational, financial, etc., in order to extend our desperate need to control. Sadly, as these evolve, they often use human beings as batteries. We created the Matrix, and without the empowering presence of human beings, any Matrix has less life than a rock. Even with the best of intentions, the Matrix is still the Matrix. We have populated the entire planet with them.

One day, a group of Matrix guardians arranged a little meeting with Jesus, ostensibly to air specific grievances they were having with the "boys in the band," the motley crew of undisciplined and uneducated disciples following Jesus. Seems this rag-tag gang of malcontents wasn't very good at keeping the rules that had long been part of the Sabbath Matrix. The religious systems forming around sacred Scriptures had effectively reduced the Word of God to a set of defensible propositions, in this particular instance revolving around the very holy subject of the day of God's rest. The Sabbath Matrix had been developed over centuries, had become increasingly complex, complete with roles, expectations, and duties, and provided a significant element of job security for the experts.

Perpetually it seemed to be a Sabbath, the holy day of the week, when Jesus ended up causing waves and in the midst of one sort of scandal or another. He would be out and about, minding his own business when stuff just. . . happened. On this day, a Sabbath of course, he and his disciples were heading somewhere and took a shortcut through a field of ripening grain. Some of them had skipped breakfast, and as they walked began snapping off heads of grain and popping them in their mouths. If you are legalistic and religious, when you are offered a gift often it is first turned into an expectation and then travels the very short distance to morph into a law. A kindness becomes a requirement.

What the legalists were out doing out on a Sabbath spying on Jesus is never recorded. Perhaps self-righteousness gives you a pass on the expectations you enforce on others. The disciples had violated a number of Sabbath rules, like harvesting and preparing a meal, so Jesus is confronted with accusation.

Keep in mind that Jesus is God comfortable inside his own skin. And Jesus deeply cares as much for these "protectors of the Holy" as he does for all those they are trying to turn into batteries. So, with a twinkle in his eye and in one sentence, he dismantles the entire cosmos as we have known it and reveals that our perception of truth is fundamentally a lie.

"The Human Being was not made for (to serve) the Sabbath, the Sabbath was made for (to serve) the Human Being!"

Did you see it, or did you only feel it? Everything changed.

The Human Being was not made for (to serve) the Matrix; any Matrix is made for (to serve) the Human Being.

The Human Being was not made for (to serve the Matrix of...) marriage, marriage was made for (to serve) the Human Being.

Incrementally, as the dawn approaches so too does the realization that "you" are more essential and significant than singleness or any institution of marriage or Matrix that has been constructed in, for, and by you. These exist to serve you (plural), not you them, and for them to do that well they must be authentic expressions of who you uniquely are. How your particular marriage is framed, for example, must be re-formed and changed as you change. Apart from the life of the butterfly itself, the chrysalis has no purpose or reason for existing. To believe otherwise is to grossly underestimate the grandeur of your humanity. Having established this, we can begin a coherent conversation about each Matrix, even the Matrix of marriage.

While I was writing this foreword, I had a phone conversation with a young man. He had sabotaged and violated his first marriage and rippled loss into the hearts of his children and into his intricately woven network of relationships, all because the imagination of another woman seemed more real than the work of his relationship with his wife. The illusion offered him a way to run. Once the infatuation had worn off and this escape hadn't saved or changed him, he wanted to run again. The problem was figuring out how to run without dragging his damage and dysfunction with him.

Marriage was never intended to be a Matrix. Before the fall marriage was another word for the relationship of the Father, Son, and Holy Spirit. Their relationship is also the definition of "Church." A few hundred years after John the Apostle penned the Revelation of Jesus, members of the faith community following Jesus crafted a word to try and describe the beauty and oneness of the being of God, or as my friend Ravi would describe it, ". . . unity and diversity in the community of the Trinity." The word they coined is *perichoresis*. Essentially, the word means the "mutual interpenetration of one with the other without the loss of personhood." Three distinct Persons in such an interpenetrated oneness with each other that the only way you can describe Them is Oneness. Not absorption, nor diminishment, but celebration. The Father never becomes the Son, nor the Son the Father, nor the Holy Spirit the Father, etc. Each is known and fully known, seen and fully seen, free in distinctiveness and in unity, the wild and free expressions of love "in" each other, grounded in the knowing of each with the others.

Humanity "turns away" from Trinity, first by Adam through choice and then by Eve through deception. To turn away is to cast your own shadow, and in that darkness reality and relationships are re-defined, violated, and diminished, and ultimately replaced by some form of Matrix. We see each other as shadow people without substance enough to make us whole, so we continue to search, turning to anything that might make us whole, or promises to. We hide in the shadows fearing it might be revealed that we ourselves are less than real, or good, or human. The shadow of self-referential incoherence.

And what did we hope to find in our turning? Identity, worth, value, significance, security, meaning, purpose, destiny, community, and love, all that we had sufficiently and fully in our face-to-face relationship with Trinity. The call of Love is not to keep looking in the shadows but to "re-turn." Fear and shame keep our faces turned away and toward the ground, so

Love enters even the shadow world and even the Matrix, and Love confronts us face to face.

Any system of hierarchy, while initially easier to navigate than authentic relationships, ultimately shutters the uniqueness of all participants, inhibits creativity, stunts personal growth and development, and fundamentally destroys the mystery of what it means to be human.

— *Wm. Paul Young*
Author of *The Shack*

INTRODUCTION

Assisting couples and organizations in creating oneness and a harmonious partnership is a rewarding and renewing experience for me. When their personal and work relationships are in tatters due to broken promises, unmet longings, and chronic disappointments it takes a lot of creativity, hope, and skill to heal wounded, fractured relationships and cultures. As a marriage therapist and leadership coach who specializes in working with egalitarian couples and collaborative-minded organizations, I believe it is more challenging to live with principles of equity than to choose a hierarchical model for either. Yet, it is the marriages and homes that subconsciously or consciously often set the tone and the values for the workplaces, companies, and churches for how men and women are to lead and work together.

Living in mutuality requires negotiating conversations, learning new conflict resolution skills, developing friendliness, and engaging in vulnerable communication. Working to establish equity is no easy task in a relationship as it requires much communication, understanding, trust, and forgiveness. This has never been an easy task between men and women and promises job security for me as an idealist who believes men

1

and women need to continue to create a new way of interacting that brings out the best in each so a synergetic outcome can be achieved.

Therefore, when couples work hard to have their power and control more equally established and their love restored, you can image my utter frustration when they attend church to build their spiritual life—and that church, covertly or overtly, reinforces patriarchal or hierarchical values. Or they lead and work in an organization that has designed a faulty system that continues to undermine and produce division based on gender. In fact, I believe couples are craving support as they seek to build secure relationships of equity while learning to lead and live together harmoniously. I believe men and women are tired of the division, accusations, and conflict that often consume our home and work lives. I believe we are all looking for a new way to interact with more respect, security, and trust so we can develop great marriages, organizations, and churches. We are designed for harmony and peace, and in our endeavors to have this, we have created systems and ways of leading that have created this sense of order and harmony. But when only one person, group, or gender is getting promoted and advanced, no one wins. Not even the privileged, because they lose out on what the oppressed have to offer.

I understand that patriarchalism has often been heralded as the divine leadership model in the home and church by many religious institutions—and yet I believe this could not be further from the heart of God and the gospel.

Subordination, hierarchies, fear, and shame are all outcomes of the fall. We are called to live in unity where "there is neither Jew nor Gentile, neither slave nor free, nor is there male and female, for you are all one in Christ Jesus" (Galatians 3:28). Unity, love, and grace are characteristics of the gospel, and we are failing our world when we continue to give leadership solutions that emulate the fall.

This book offers a methodology on how to develop unity and equity, and create culturally relevant systems for couples to grow, serve, and lead harmoniously together. It also provides support for marriages to develop relational equity and develop a symbiotic relationship with churches. In so doing, we create the harmonious melody of mutuality, the music of Eden, which overflows to our workplaces, churches, and communities.

Throughout all three sections of this book, the story of Adam and Eve is woven into the readings to entertain, inspire, and compel the reader to visualize an age-old issue through a new lens.

We will imagine, "What if Adam and Eve went to church after the fall? What church would best represent their perfect little life before sin entered it? How do they return to Eden in their marriage and experience garden living once again? Having experienced Eden living, what would Adam and Eve require in their marriage and in a church to thrive again?"

And in answering these questions, we will discover what we need to thrive as well.

When we choose to live, breathe, and minister under the effects of sin, we are bringing division at every turn, and cultivating a breeding ground for chaos and disaster to be harvested. Love cultivates a fertile soil where relationships can be restored, hope renewed, and faith replenished in order to move mountains. We are made for more, for perfection, and to live harmoniously in love. Through the reversing effects of the cross, we now have a choice to move in an upward spiral that takes us closer to our Creator and embodies his redemptive work, or to continue in the downward spiral initiated by the crippling effects of sin. Bringing some heaven to earth sounds much more appealing to me as I choose to cultivate the transforming language of love in my life and with others desiring harmonious community.

Relationship Remodel with the Change Cycle

Create in me a clean heart O God and renew a right spirit within me. (Psalms 51:10)

I believe we were made to create like our Creator.

When God created the earth, he did some cleaning and started organizing the inky, black space, a "soup of nothingness, a bottomless emptiness, an inky blackness" (Genesis 1:1-2 MSG). He rolled up his sleeves, turned on the light, and began to work with what he had. He created order for the earth to handle the fantastic creation awaiting it. For the first three days he just separated light from dark and day from night, bodies of waters, heavens from the waters, and land from seas, and lastly spoke the vegetation into being.

It wasn't till the fourth day he really got busy and created some serious light with the sun and moon so he could set about creating all the life we see today, in the ocean, land, and skies, including his crown of creation, humankind. Every day revealed new life that seemed to be a dramatic crescendo to the ultimate life creation, humans made in OUR image, or the image of a triune God. After three magnificent days of artistry, he admired what he masterfully created and like a skilled, expert artist he proclaimed, *"It is good! So very, very good!"* Like the drumroll that cues the resounding cymbals of an arousing symphony coming to its completion, he conducted the ultimate masterpiece, proclaimed its finality, dropped his arms, closed his mouth, and stopped speaking creation into being, then . . . he rested.

We were made to create in every area of our lives. And it is through creating that we lead, transform our lives and relationships, and invent new things. When we create, we renew our lives and rejuvenate our world. When we create, we relate to ourselves, our loved ones, and our world. Our new creations are renewing, refreshing, and rejuvenating for us and those around us. When we don't create, we lose the ability to speak beauty into chaos, as well as the superb confidence that comes from transforming nothing into majesty. This is who our God is. The Great Recycler who uses everything and everyone to bring heaven to earth in all our relationships—our marriages, families, workplace, and communities.

When we create, we relate better, and celebrate community best. The most challenging part is creating something out of nothing, order out of chaos, light from darkness, and beauty from ashes. Like the God whose image we were made in, we need the cleansing light to penetrate the darkness so we can see a vision bigger than ourselves, the passion and faith to speak and create life into being where there was none, and the courage to be content with our creation. We must find a sense of completion in an ever-changing world and to choose rest.

Yet, I often wonder how God rested when he knew what he created would ultimately demand the life of his son to save the precious creation he made. This tells me that resting must be a choice when greatness has been achieved even if the greatness will not last.

In the emerging field of Positive Psychology, optimism and hope are used to facilitate change. The therapist capitalizes on the strengths of an individual in order to foster change, while the diagnosis plays a small role in treating the individual. Viewing the person through their strengths versus their diagnosis or inadequacies dramatically impacts the dynamics of the whole therapy process, as the focus is on the solution instead of the problem.

Having practiced both techniques, I have found it fulfilling and rewarding to diagnose the presenting problem then move to the plausible solutions or technique to solve their problem. Otherwise, the client or organization can get stuck in this quagmire of guilt, hopelessness, defeat, hurt, and unresolved shame, which only contributes more to the common presenting issues of anxiety and depression. I describe this as the FOG of dysfunction as they spin in their Fear, Obligation, and Guilt.

I believe people can remodel their relationships instead of replacing them. To be sure, it is not for the faint of heart, and requires vision, faith, and courage to identify how to accomplish a relationship remodel. Therefore, I developed an easy-to-recall system based on the Creation model for people to do a Relationship Remodel in their marriages, other close relationships, and communities, and create the life they want. Here's the three-step Change Cycle, which is much easier to remember than implement:

I. CLEAN negative, unwanted, or outdated behavior and choices out of your space

II. CREATE positive or clean changes to achieve the life of peace and love you desire

III. COMPLETE the remodel and experience peaceful, loving relationships and healthy cultures

For instance, if I want to change some communication issues, first I identify what needs to be cleaned out: CLEAN out by identifying negative, critical communication hurting my relationships.

Then I identify what I want to create: CREATE positive, clear communication by stating what I feel and need without criticizing.

Finally, I envision what my relationships will look like if I take the time to remodel my communication: COMPLETE the communication changes and experience peaceful, loving relationships where we can have more positive feelings and pleasant interactions.

A few questions are asked for each section in this three-step process:

CLEAN - Turn the light on: what is the truth of the issue?
Describe: What do we want to change?
Purpose: Why do we want this changed?

CREATE - Speak the truth into being: what is your vision?
Describe: What do we want to create?
Strategy: How will we do this?

COMPLETE - Celebrate what you completed: what did you accomplish?

Describe: What is the final outcome you want to celebrate?

Analysis: How do you want to maintain and improve what you've created?

When we are able to implement the Change Cycle, we are able to do a Relationship Remodel and experience our best life in our homes, work, and churches. To create clarity and ease for the reader, this book is separated into three sections: Clean, Create, and Complete, and will help to guide you as I address creating a Relationship Remodel for marriages and churches.

Marriages and the church might not be heaven, but they are designed to be the intermediate space where we get to experience a little bit of heaven on earth, if and only if we choose to speak and live in love, harmony and equity. If we are not experiencing love in our marriages, we need to re-evaluate what is causing our inability to share and receive love. If we are not experiencing loving, harmonious community in the church, we may want to ask: what is our purpose, and what is preventing us from living in love? The church needs to be the leading exemplars in developing unity and harmony among the genders. Anything less does not embody the heart and mind of our God who is the ultimate embodiment of love.

Couples in contemporary marriages are figuring out how to navigate cultural changes and shifting family dynamics, and live with equity. They are called Peer Marriages, and church cultures can learn much from these couples who are learning to forge deep friendships, partner equitably, and lead with love.

Leadership expert David Livermore writes, "Of all the cultural systems, the family system is widely regarded as the single most important system to understand, but this information often feels irrelevant to many organizational leaders."[1] Understanding and appreciating how our modern marriages are working provides insight and awareness for how organizations can also develop in a positive way.

Heterosexual marriages are the focus of this book, which is not an attempt to exclude or marginalize same-sex marriages. Rather, it is an attempt to identify the perpetual struggle between the genders often starting in heterosexual marriages that gets carried over to churches and workplaces. *Reclaiming Eden* teaches how to resolve competitive tensions better in the home so as to bring more respectful relationships between the genders in the church and into other communities.

Hopefully, *Reclaiming Eden* opens up your hearts and minds to start healthy dialogues grounded in truth. And as we speak cultures of unity into being between the genders in the church and home, we cultivate a space for love, joy, and peace to grow that is beneficial to all relationships. Thus we create a bit of heaven here on earth reminiscent of the garden from which we came and the paradise to which we are going.

SECTION 1
CLEAN | EDEN AWAITS

CHAPTER 1

My Story

My Marriage Story

Jake and I met in our freshman year at Azusa Pacific University in Southern California. We were both eighteen and became fast friends.

I knew right away what I wanted to do with my life and was studying to be an educator. Jake was another story. Through most of his college career, he was undecided about what he wanted to pursue. At the last minute, he declared a ministry degree and pursued youth ministry, taking an internship position at a local church.

Being his friend, I offered to work with him to develop his program and lead girls' groups. I was also curious if this was the age group I wanted to work with or teach as I was not satisfied with my elementary education experience.

Jake was one of the best youth pastors and administrators I have ever worked with. His charisma, charm, enthusiastic, uninhibited personality, athleticism, good looks, combined with his deep faith, great administrative abilities, and leadership skills made him a natural for the position. Kids, adults, and staff just loved him.

For months, we worked together, and had a great time using our strengths and abilities to complement one another, partner collaboratively, and find our stride individually as we worked together as a unit.

Working in the Church of God, there were no gender restrictions, and I led, preached, started a youth band, and served in whatever capacity I felt passionate and gifted in. This was a very freeing and wonderful experience for me as we worked collaboratively together, unrestricted by gender and supported by the pastoral leadership. We had no idea how unusual this was, and years later would often look back longingly at these special days as being the marriage ideal.

Jake, moved by my contribution and partnership, paid me half of his monthly internship stipend. Ceremoniously, he would make out a "Payday" card with some of my favorite treats and leave it on my desk at work with half of his paycheck. He reasoned, "Why should I be getting all the pay when Jenn is doing half of the work?"

In the process, we fell in love. Our ministry partnership in Southern California had gone so well, we not only wanted to build a future together, we wanted to co-minister together.

The Jake and Jenn partnership was born, as we married a year and a half later, and pursued a new life in Cottage Grove, Oregon. Jake found employment at a church as a youth pastor and I took a teaching job in Eugene, Oregon.

Unbeknownst to us, mixing marriage and ministry would become a game-changer. What had been an easy, rewarding partnership slowly developed into a frustrating, confusing relationship for us.

The Root of the Problem

To understand the painful development, we had to retrace our steps to our education. When Jake received his education, he was drilled on the importance of honoring his calling to ministry above all else and to consider his calling to full-time ministry his true vocation. He was taught that ministry was the sacred chalice from which only those "called" could drink from, rendering these chosen ones above all others as they pursued their sacred vocation as a minister.

This was news to me! I never understood this philosophy of this exclusive ministry teaching. For me, being one with God is not synonymous with being one with your calling, yet there was no differentiation between the two in Jake's education. According to Jake, creating oneness with your marriage partner was never discussed, taught, or emphasized, as your ministry calling trumped all else.

In other words, unbeknownst to me, I had fallen in love with a man who put his calling above all else at the direct teaching of his ministry program.

This was a precarious foundation for any marriage to start on.

I can't say I never saw any signs.

Not at first, of course. During Jake's internship, I'd felt a true partnership and equality as we worked side by side. At one point during our engagement, however, Jake and I found ourselves talking about gender discrimination and the "two-for-one" mentality many pastors' wives experienced. When I told him I wanted no part of this, he stressed the importance of his calling over mine (and over me!) and for a short period of time, I broke off our engagement.

Looking back, we should have explored this further but, regrettably, we thought love was enough and decided God—who had clearly brought us together—would work this all out in the future.

Today, as marriage therapists, we look back at our younger selves and yell, "WHAT THE BLEEP WERE WE THINKING??"

But at the time, we were young, naive, and in love.

A Painful Journey

Still newlyweds, we moved to Tri-Cities, Washington, where Jake assumed another youth pastor position then later advanced into an administrative pastor position. I started a middle school teaching position at a private school, and we both went back to graduate school for our master's degrees in Social Work for clinical counseling.

The young church grew from 100 to over 700 in the seven years we were there, and we have so many fun memories and relationships from that thriving era.

But the demanding work and exclusive pastoral partnership created a slow divide for us, as the church, staff, and his calling eclipsed Jake's time, attention, and partnership with me.

Although Jake valued my personal calling as an educator, and later as a therapist, he struggled to affirm it if it interfered with his work.

Remember, I did not drink from the sacred chalice of being "called." We fought frequently on creating unity together, never really aware of the underlying theme of our marriage we were constantly attempting to navigate: Jake's calling mattered most.

As the church covertly placed more importance on the calling and profession of the male—thus placing me at a distant second—both Jake and I felt the change from our dating years.

Jake grieved this loss of partnership and equity, as I did. To compensate, he supported me well in my teacher role, grading papers, helping in the classroom, and even subbing for me. He also deeply honored my desire to not be treated as an addition to his pastoral position and advocated for me with others when gender stereotypes were placed on me. For instance, he never assumed we were partners in ministry, and intentionally pursued other volunteer help to communicate to the church that I had my own vocation. When I chose to help, Jake wanted the church leadership to view me as a volunteer and treat me with the same respect and honor. To prove this point, when Jake honored volunteers with gifts and accolades, he always included me, to the chagrin of other staff spouses who felt responsible for fulfilling half of the roles of their pastoral partners.

Problem was, I wanted to be more than a volunteer. I wanted to be an equal partner with him.

In our efforts to create boundaries and some individuation with the church, we lost the magic of us in our partnership and unity. We missed *us*. We missed the freedom of operating in our giftedness, oblivious to gender roles and pastoral stereotypes.

We missed the dynamics of working with our best friend. We missed the shared passion, purpose, and unity of mind. But most of all, we missed the power and control to be who we wanted, and to be treated with respect and equity, regardless of our gender or marriage status.

After having our two kids, McKenna and Dawson, we entered an even more confusing and conflicted state. We both wanted to parent, do ministry, and work as we provided and parented. I initially thought I wanted to be a stay-at-home mom, and I completed my schooling for counseling just in time to stay home and mother. This lasted for two years before I started becoming restless and desired to build my counseling career. Jake was progressing in his pastor position and was also on a national team traveling the country, while I was "stuck" at home. Ironically, he missed the home life and raising the kids, and although I loved mothering, I missed the professional world. The psychological sadness of missing "us" and being trapped in a world that didn't suit us was hijacking our love and partnership together, as fear and confusion took forerunner. Conflict increased as the demands from Jake's work continued to divide us.

The church we attended and Jake pastored gave us mixed messages about gender parity and equity. It was a Church of God out of Anderson, Indiana, and was started by a woman, with many prominent positions within the network held by women. Yet, female pastoring seemed unwanted, irrelevant, and devalued as traditional gender roles were reinforced.

One Sunday morning when they were short ushers for the offering, I saw their dilemma and cheerfully volunteered to do it. The men present stared at me shocked then chuckled, looked over my head at one another, and said snidely, "The day a woman does the offering is the day I stop."

I was stunned at the blatant disrespect and their strong commitment to reinforcing gender roles.

Another time in an annual church meeting, I politely requested they consider adding a female pastor to our all-male staff to offer support for youth and women congregants. A male usher elbowed my husband telling him to get me "back in line, to which Jake responded, "She's just fine." In the seven years of attending the church, I heard a woman preach only twice, and she was the female music minister who was on staff. She eventually left—or some would say "got driven out"—and no female pastor has ever replaced her since. That was over twenty years ago, and the church is currently over 2,000 members with all male ministers.

Jake attempted to get female leaders' voices in the main service and asked any woman willing to participate. Most would not even consider speaking, so he found other ways to involve them by asking them to pray or do announcements. He once asked a prominent, deeply respected woman theologian to pray in the main service. With much hesitation, she agreed, but Jake feared she would break an ankle judging by how hard she trembled in her heels as she prayed in a shaky and terrified voice! She later explained she did not feel women should take the stage in the Sunday service even though she taught the weekly women's Bible study on the same stage.

This was overt gender discrimination, but covert messages were constant and undermining of females and their leadership.

Women were intimidated and blocked from leading, directing, preaching, and in any area outside of the traditional gender roles in a church association that was started by a woman and ordained women ministers! How did this happen, and why did I constantly feel like I was breaking the rules and being chided to step back in line?

Tragically, it was not just women who experienced the discrimination, but minorities as well. Once, I naively invited a Hispanic co-worker to come to church with me, and not one person approached her or greeted her. It broke my heart when she walked out and said to me, "Don't ever do that to me again." Church was a humiliating experience for her, and the discriminatory spirit that I sensed and felt in the church further angered me.

This dark spirit confirmed its presence once again when I was at a church function standing in line for cake. I heard the man next to me say, while gesturing to the African-American couple I adored, "What are those n****** doing here?" In complete shock, I turned and looked at him, thinking my ears had failed me, and he unabashedly stared back. Growing up in Southern California, I had not experienced such overt discrimination. It completely shocked me and left me speechless.

In the meantime, our kids had come fast and furiously, only fourteen months apart and requiring two traumatic c-sections. Between raising two toddlers and the stress of our lives—and recovering from past unresolved childhood abuse—my physical and emotional health started to spiral downward. Depression, frustration, and despair spun me in circles.

For the first time in my life, I sought ongoing medical and therapeutic attention for chronic sickness and deteriorating health. A doctor I visited later recounted to me that when she saw me, she thought I was dying from a thyroid disorder and had secretly prayed for me for three months! I felt miserable physically.

I also felt miserable emotionally as I continued to ward off the invalidating, undermining messages that were marginalizing me and keeping me confined to gender expectations in my church community. Women continued to be seen but not heard in the main service, and I craved the spiritual wisdom of my kind. Roles were too often assigned by gender, and benevolent sexism where only certain types of women were advanced was evident. If only I could have smiled sweetly and deferred demurely to male leaders like I once had, I could have led more and been promoted.

But, intuitively, I was sick of doing this, and I couldn't stomach the charade anymore. I wanted to be freely and fiercely me. The mixed messages of ordaining women pastors and female leaders—yet not advancing or mentoring women— created instability and frustration in me. I hated to disappoint people, and I was constantly torn between pleasing others and pursuing myself. I knew what I wanted and needed, but I felt lost in how to create it as my life force seemed to be slipping quickly away.

I felt like I was a chronic disappointment to my husband, my church, and my God.

After five years of this, I felt like I couldn't take one more minute of this distressing nightmare.

One Sunday, in the middle of service, I leaned over to Jake and told him to pick up the kids. Then I stood and walked right down the aisle and out the door.

CHAPTER 2

The Awakening

After walking out, I drove myself to my sanctuary as I held my own church service by the river, and I had a real "come to Jesus" meeting. I wasn't mad at him I was just so alone and confused about what to do. I remember saying to him, "I think you made a mistake with me."

Just as quickly, I heard him speak in my spirit. *I don't make mistakes. I trust you.*

I thought he had a good point about not making mistakes, but I questioned if I had heard him correctly on how he trusted me. God trusting *me?* It was a new idea, and one that had never been taught to me—I'd only learned how we should trust God.

Then just as quickly I saw the whole Bible flip through all its stories, as I heard him in my spirit say, *What about in the garden when I made the tree of good and evil? I trusted humans to make the right choice.* In seconds, God took me through all the Old Testament Bible stories, showing me how he trusted and worked with humans. He continued until showing me the ultimate example of trusting Mary to carry, birth, nurse, and nurture God in human form, Jesus.

This was my paradigm shift, and I remember thinking, *If God trusts me, maybe I should learn how to trust myself.*

That was a turning point as I began to develop a stronger partnership with God, learning how to hear his voice through my feelings, spirit, and thoughts.

God became my constant source of comfort, and today I look back at that time as a cleaning-out process. He was developing me to be who he made me to be instead of what the church wanted me to be.

During this time, I started having powerful dreams in which I was being attacked, drowned, and killed. Just as startling were other dreams about how God really saw me. In these dreams, he literally gave me a new name and a new image of myself in a powerful Indian chieftess dream that still guides me to this day.

I started to make a shift from who I *thought* I was to who I *really* was.

When I told Jake I needed to leave this community, he said I couldn't or I'd ruin his career. He was right, and we both knew it. We were in a system that valued him at the expense of me. In our community, I was needed to support him, but I was not needed for what I had to offer. How was this ever okay for him? For me? For us? How did we get here?

But here we were with no quick solutions, so I stayed for another two years, while quietly planning my—and hopefully our—escape. I knew I had to leave this dysfunction behind,

but I wanted to leave without creating too much upheaval—
and I wanted my marriage too.

The Shift

I longed to partner collaboratively with Jake in providing
and parenting, and I wanted to be respected and treated as an
equal in my church.

Jake wanted to pursue the pastoral position he loved and
do more parenting with the kids he adored.

After much "discussion" (tears, anger, conflicts. . .) we
again attempted to go back to our original goal of working and
doing life together. I opened up my therapy business and was
experiencing rapid growth. In the meantime, Jake asked the
church if he could work part time so he could both pastor and
parent. After eight months of deliberating, the church refused
his request to hold his pastoral position at a part-time capacity.

The bold ones chided me for "taking him away from his
calling" and for "not respecting his position," and my favorite,
"not being a team player." The more subdued members
mumbled behind my back, shooting me disapproving looks
and politely distancing from me.

I struggled with guilt, shame, and hurt and vowed if I ever
got an opportunity to address this injustice, I would so I could
help create a more accepting church space for couples like us.

We get it. We never did fit the ideal pastor and pastor's wife
role. We love God, people, and helping the hurting, we just
love doing it in partnership and in an equitable culture. We are
both dynamic, charismatic individuals, and as middle children,
neither one of us does well being sidelined by others. What a

refreshing disappointment we must have been—empowering to some and frustrating to others as we tried to break the stained-glass ceiling for both genders in church ministry.

The Road to Healing

While Jake was still employed at the church, we began applying for co-ministry positions around the US, but they kept trying to put me under his leadership, using words and phrases like "headship," "pursuing his calling," "under his covering," and "final authority." And here's the kicker: these were egalitarian churches who believed in the equity of men and women ministers!

With our BA degrees, years of Christian education, and master's degrees, we knew we were more qualified and educated than many denominational pastors, but we also knew we were offering a different way of doing ministry the church did not want. Jake was in high demand and had to repeatedly turn down respectable church offers due to their discriminatory stance on women leaders.

Tragically, the church at large became a demeaning, demanding, and divisive voice that was threatening to tear us apart, and it could not offer us a viable work model that showed professional courtesy and respect to us both. It became a culturally delayed and irrelevant ethos for our partnering marriage.

After several attempts at finding co-pastoring positions, we gave up. Jake's "ministry calling" could not trump my calling, and we saw no room for us in the ministry profession.

With two small kids and a new house mortgage, Jake wept as he gave notice and walked away from his beloved pastoral position. In seven years, the church had become a thriving place in our community and it was all the friends and family we had in the area.

We were shell-shocked, devastated, and heart-broken. We had both dumped so much of ourselves into the lives and families of the congregation, and we knew many were confused and felt abandoned at our misrepresented and misunderstood departure. In our desperation of feeling entirely alone, alienated, and gasping for the air to emotionally thrive, we did a few things: we *finally* went to counseling (better late than never), we educated ourselves, and we stayed away from damaging "Christian" cultures and messages.

And in the process, we discovered an amazing woman pastor and licensed therapist who helped dust us off and put us back on our feet. We had prayer warriors pray over us. We cried and went to a class to learn how to comfort each other. I went to therapy to deal with the effects of post-traumatic stress and trauma. We worked more on bonding in love instead of fear. We also educated ourselves on our issue as we read books about spiritual abuse, as well as self-help and spiritual healing books. Intentionally, we stayed away from most Christian books for women, men, family, and marriage. Their messages echoed the masked patriarchalism pains we were still recovering from.

My supportive twin sister recommended two books that completely changed my paradigm as a Christian woman. One spoke to my personal healing and development, *The Dance of the Dissident Daughter* by Sue Monk Kidd. In it, she was able to put words to what intuitively I knew but wasn't able to express. The other book, *Equal to the Task* by Ruth Haley Barton, addressed healthy relationships between men and women. Barton's book came at the perfect time and was the oxygen we needed to breathe deeply and confidently again. She promoted gender parity and partnership within the home and church, revealing how it can be done with ease and clarity.

Her words changed our lives and gave us an ideal to emulate. We pursued a partnership in the home and work as we started our own therapy business. Jake worked construction for a year as he joined my therapy practice, running from the construction site to the office. We would exchange the kids in the parking lot while one would go counsel, and the other would go home to parent. We were living the dream!

We now know we were pursuing the Peer Marriage model where we both were providing and parenting. Years later we discovered the book *Peer Marriages* by Dr. Pepper Schwartz that came to define our marriage and the expertise in our marital therapy practice today.

Entering into the world of therapy provided more opportunity, earning potential, ministry, equitable treatment, and partnership for Jake and me. We are able to speak, counsel, do workshops, advocate for justice, and write about issues plaguing our communities—all as equals.

It has been twenty years since Jake left church ministry, and we have raised our kids in a God-centered home with a Peer Marriage in the best way we knew how. If there is one thing I have learned through my journey, all members need to be considered equal, and justice must be established in order to create unity in the body of Christ.

A Shared Vision

My marriage story is my greatest reason for writing this book. Jake and I also have tragically discovered it echoes the stories of many others -women discriminated from church leadership and marriages frustrated with mixed messages of gender parity.

We are needed to be the rational voice of reason in a world that has become unreasonable and irrational in how to treat the opposite gender.

If a couple has agreed to partner together, to parent and provide without hierarchies, churches need to support and model this. It is not only scripturally accurate but also culturally relevant for modern marriages.

Marriage is hard enough without having to navigate gender power struggles, discrimination, and mistreatment from well-meaning church leaders. The church needs healthy marriages, and the church needs to be about assisting marriages to live their best lives in love, unity, and a harmonious partnership.

The church has the answers for a viable solution to create unity, and now is the time to come together to create a just system so we can implement the scriptural principles of equity.

My marriage needed a just culture of equity then, and it needs it now.

Martin Luther King, Jr., could not have established unity if there had not first been a united vision and a just system to support it. Too often we struggle to offer a just system in churches to support gender parity because we are too hung up on reinforcing bygone gender stereotypes meant for another era. We must take the gospel of equity into this century and present a gospel that brings the good news to a world hungry for the melody of mutuality among the genders.

This is the good news: creating a community built on love and the principles that bring a unified, peaceful community changes our marriages and our world, and reflects the heart of God. Getting lost in a doctrine that does anything less is reminiscent of the church of yesteryear that ended up crucifying the One who came to bring the abundant life we all crave.

My Dream

I have a dream of something better, a culture where men and women are operating harmoniously together, and where the church is the leading example of this in our fractured world.

But to achieve this dream, we need to write a new story. Thankfully, we know exactly where to find the inspiration for what this should look like and to discover God's heart on the matter. To write this new story, we need a new narrative that isn't new at all.

In fact, it takes us back to the beginning, back to a time before darkness got its talons into our hearts.

CHAPTER 3

God's Original Design

Then God said, *"Let us make mankind in our image, in our likeness, so that they may rule over the fish in the sea and the birds in the sky, over the livestock and all the wild animals, and over all the creatures that move along the ground."*
So God created mankind in his own image, in the image of God he created them; male and female he created them. God blessed them and said to them, *'Be fruitful and increase in number; fill the earth and subdue it. Rule over the fish in the sea and the birds in the sky and over every living creature that moves on the ground."* (Genesis 1:26-28)

I like to imagine: *What if Adam and Eve went to church before the fall? What church would they choose to attend? What church would best represent their perfect little life before sin entered it?*

In reality, they were the first and last perfect church. Just the two of them, reflecting and relating to their perfect friend and Creator, God.

Before the fall, Adam and Eve were having a great ol' time! They were ruling creation together, enjoying evening walks with their Creator, riding the lions, and romping around naked with no ability to feel shame. They felt no pain, knew no death, experienced no fear, and work was enjoyable but not necessary. Food was plentiful and grew unhindered and unassisted.

It was like a permanent vacation at one of the most luxurious, all-inclusive resorts you can imagine, and then even much, much better. They ate, played, ruled together as one, and enjoyed their Creator as he walked and talked among them. Love, joy, and peace were the predominant emotions. Adam and Eve were in their divine element, truly living heaven on earth.

Who knows how long they lived this way? Perhaps it was days, months, or centuries.

But at some point, their days of perfection tragically came to a close. The wretched day came when they were both deceived, and shame, fear, and death ensued. A hierarchy was established between the two, pain became their constant companion, and work became mandatory to live.

They were banished from their perfect, beautiful paradise, forced to live clothed, perpetually navigating shame and alienated from their Creator and each other.

This must have been a private hell on earth for these two.

With the help of God, Eve survived the birth of her first-born, Cain, who became the first murderer to roam the earth after killing his brother, Abel. This is every parent's nightmare for their child—and to make matters worse, any dreams and hopes for reconciliation were dashed as Cain was banished to wander the earth.

With two sons lost, Adam and Eve pressed on in a life that must have felt painfully dreary compared to the perfection they once knew. Imagine living in perfection, connection, and love, and then being reduced to living in pain, fear, and death.

And just as sin entered the world, so did a great divide between relationships. How many times did they kick themselves for their new existence, wishing they could go back to their paradise for just a day?

I imagine that sometimes they must have relived the glory days, reminiscing about life before the fall. I wonder how they managed to live joyfully from then on. In fact, perhaps the angst they must have felt—the chronic shame of losing everything they'd once had—sped up the effects of evil consuming the earth.

Whatever the contributing factors may have been, the reality is that earth and its inhabitants atrophied so quickly and horribly that eventually God regretted ever making humans. He pushed a reset button. Flooded the earth. Started all over with a single family headed by Noah. In Genesis 6:7-8 (The MSG) it says: "God saw that human evil was out of control. People thought evil, imagined evil—evil, evil, evil from morning to night. God was sorry that he had made the human race in the first place; it broke his heart. God said, "I'll get rid of my ruined creation, make a clean sweep: people, animals, snakes and bugs, birds—the works. I'm sorry I made them." But Noah was different. God liked what he saw in Noah." God did a remodel of his creation, and cleaned out the icky stuff by washing it all away and created a new world through Noah.

As humans began again, God orchestrated a plan that he wove through the pages of time. Indeed, through the ministry and sacrifice of Jesus, human relationships became restored, and the curtain in the temple separating us from our holy Creator was torn from top to bottom as we were also restored to community with our Creator. Garden living reinstated once again. No more division from the One who made us to live in community with him.

Through the ministry and sacrifice of Jesus, there were no more blood sacrifices, no more going through priests to talk with God, and no more hierarchies.

In Jesus Christ, there is no longer male, female, slave or free, and we are all equal as we become one in Christ Jesus (Galatians 3:28).

As God's plan unfolded, a new community—the church—was created. In the church, we have the opportunity to recreate garden living, to come together in love and equity, to live in freedom and relationship, not quite achieving heaven on earth as Adam and Eve experienced, but getting a whole lot closer than we were living.

We have the opportunity to live the life we were literally created to live.

Learning to Pray Our Restoration

After the fall, prayer was transformed from garden walks with God to blood sacrifices orchestrated by priests.

But under the redemptive ministry of Jesus, even intimacy and equality in prayer was restored. Through the Lord's Prayer, Jesus taught us how to pray, and in the process begin to undo the effects of the fall and experience greater intimacy with God and with each other.

And he set the stage with the first words of his prayer: *Our Father. . .*

What powerful words! In fact, with a single word—*our*—he communicated that relationship with the Father belongs equally to us all, that we are to live and pray in community with one another as we love and commune with our Creator. Equity is restored, as the word *our* reminds us that he is God to us all regardless of gender, ethnicity, sexuality, class, age, or deeds done. *"Our Father, who art in heaven, hallowed be thy name. . ."*

Jesus then taught us to ask the seemingly impossible, to ask that God's will be done and that his kingdom be present on earth just as it is in Heaven: *"Thy kingdom come, thy will be done, on earth as it is in heaven. . ."* And that, I might add, takes us much closer to those days of perfection in the garden.

With his next words, Jesus called us to depend on our Father—as we once did so fully in the garden—by asking him for our daily bread. *"Give us this day our daily bread. . ."* Again, this is a beautiful picture of dependence on him rather than on the labor and toil that was instituted at the fall.

From there, Jesus addressed the restoration of relationships by teaching us to pray, *"Forgive us our debts as we forgive our debtors. . ."* Again, we see how unity and relational restoration is promoted through the forgiveness of one another and ourselves. He taught us that we can now go directly to God and ask forgiveness of our trespasses, eliminating the need for the hierarchal intervention of priests. We are instructed to let forgiveness be given and received laterally among ourselves.

He then taught us to pray these words: *"And lead us not into temptation, but deliver us from evil. . ."* I imagine these words as God's personal help hotline to be used when we become tempted to repeat the mistakes of Adam and Eve, becoming deceived or disobedient. When these things happen, we get to ask for deliverance.

Jesus' final words proclaim an earth restored: *"For thine is the kingdom, and the power, and the glory, forever."* Basically, God wins, has always won, and will always win, FOREVER, no matter what. We are on the winning team, for all eternity. We may have lost the garden for now, but we can regain a semblance of it on earth through his church and can look forward to perfect garden living in eternity. We cannot lose with him.

The Lord's Prayer[1] is really a restoration prayer in light of all that was stolen from us in the garden.

When we reject his original design, we continue to experience the devastating effects of broken, conflicted relationships consumed with death, shame, and fear. We deny the resurrection power of Jesus to redeem and restore all things.

The Lord's Prayer defiantly protests the work of sin. And in this one simple prayer, Jesus reminds us who God is and what we now have a right to ask for once again.

Living God's Original Design Today

So how exactly do we begin to experience garden living in an imperfect world?

We need to invite heaven to earth and go back to praying for the culture of Eden to permeate our lives, marriages, churches, and communities. We get to ask that heaven comes to earth through our relationships. We must stop rehearsing and practicing the fall and live in the faith and wonder of a new world being created and restored daily through the loving, grace-filled restoration process of OUR compassionate Creator.

OUR Father has invited us to ask him to bring heaven to earth. This is the ultimate sign of trust restored as he covets a deep relationship with his creation.

Asking questions like "What kind of marriage did Adam and Eve experience in the early garden days, and what church would they want to attend?" keeps us inspired to recreate the garden days.

We've been creating marriages and churches based on the fall, and in the process fostering a culture of death, shame, division, and fear. Instead of maintaining and emulating the effects of sin, let's dream about bringing heaven to earth again in ALL marriages, churches, and communities as we ask God's will to be done.

There is the real Adam and Eve from the garden days, and then there is the synthetic or counterfeit Adam and Eve from the fall. We need to model our relationships on the real deal. Not a facsimile but the real, authentic, perfect male and female who modeled perfect community between the genders.

Although some consider this the perfect marital design, I consider it more than that. This was the original design for community between the genders and among humans—and it's a design that our world desperately needs.

Jesus never made fakes. He was the real deal and made the original designs for greatness. And he is the One who can help us recreate his one-of-a kind, original design in our lives and our relationships today.

We may never achieve the complete original design this side of heaven but using the original design as our model will help us get so much closer than continuing to use the downgraded model of Adam and Eve as our blueprint for marriages and churches.

We must turn our attention to the ancient, original community, marriage, and mini-church God created with Adam and Eve in the garden—and use that model for creating healthy marriages, churches, and communities today.

This is not a proclamation about the perfect gender-mixed, heterosexual marriage but rather it is a call beckoning us back to how community needs to be among the genders and humans, with the original woman and man.

Regardless of sexual orientation, religious preference, or ethnicity, we can all benefit from how men and women were designed to interact in the home, at work, and in spiritual communities. We are not called to use, abuse, or objectify one another. Quite the opposite. We are designed to love, adore, cherish, and rule harmoniously together.

Like a great recipe of old, this has been passed down through the ages, and through the redemptive work of Jesus and his life modeling, we are able to experience restoration of the original loving and equitable community between man and woman.

Ah, the way things were meant to be.

A Vision of Gender Parity

Living in hierarchy under and above one another is keeping the curtain in place and denying us entrance to the holy places with each other and God. We are all called to be priests and can all access the throne of God because of the ultimate sacrifice that ended all sacrifices. Introducing a hierarchy in marriage or within the church defies the redeeming, reconciling, work God did for us to be reconciled through Jesus Christ and each other as he removed the dooming effects of sin.

If we claim the restorative work of Jesus, we can partake in the beauty of relating in grace, honor, and equity. We can be light walkers living in love with one another, channeling a God full of light and love, as we bring a bit of heaven to earth.

We can claim the freedom, love, and grace that were generously restored to us through the death and resurrection of Jesus Christ and allow his resurrection power to be revealed in our marriages, churches, and communities. Gender parity within communities based on love, grace, and equity are evidence of the redemptive work of Christ, and are ours to have if we desire it.

To keep it simple, I like to refer to the marriage model before the fall as something that any marriage can aspire to emulate, a relationship model in which humans partner powerfully and equitably together, without hierarchies or limitations.

I call this the melody of mutuality. It is the ultimate example of how both genders partner together to establish and rule a new world. This is the ultimate model I want to invite couples to embrace. Marriage really can be restored to operate under the same principles of love and equity that were in effect before the destructive effects of sin and death.

Regarding men and women ruling together, God created the perfect design by having a man and woman working together equitably and harmoniously in the garden.

We can experience this design today by unequivocally caring for each other and everything he has created as we operate together. Perfection is never the goal but rather progress to reclaiming what we were designed to be.

An inevitable experience in life for every person on the planet is the experience of relating to someone from the opposite sex. I am a mother to a son, daughter to a father, sister to a brother, and wife to a husband.

In other words, men influence and shape every sphere of my existence. I want to honor and value them. I want to protect, nurture, love, respect, and partner with them. I just want that same honor and value returned. I want a relationship of reciprocity. A relationship that allows us to stand next to each other instead of in front or over each other, and where equity becomes the mode of operation for all.

I want "power with" instead of a "power over" as we lead collaboratively with a shared vision of developing a culture of equity where it is possible to reinstate garden living for all. I want to give birth and nurture the life produced from the seeds men plant. I want good seeds planted by great men so I can partner in harvesting a great crop. I do not want to tend the weeds of patriarchalism, inequity, and fear anymore. These seeds will never produce a great harvest.

Men and women, personally and professionally, overlap each other in relationships and we all have similar longings to be loved, appreciated, respected, and accepted. When there are hierarchies based on genders, whether unintentional or intentional, it is difficult if not impossible to cultivate a culture for all to be valued as equals.

As Jesus followers, we are to be leaders in creating healthy communities full of equity, unity, and diversity, offering a replica of the sweet garden days. For churches in America, now is the time to write a new narrative for how the genders can work better together in unity with diversity. And in doing so, we can create a healthy model for a hurting world longing for peaceful, authentic community.

Where there is no vision for gender unity there will be no direction forward in creating gender harmony, and no stable ethos for us to be the people of peace we are called to be.

Where there is no vision for gender unity, we pour our energies instead into navigating double binds and confusing mixed messages instead of working better together to make a positive impact on our world.

We need each other and the world needs models of men and women working collaboratively together in the homes and churches.

Whether a small church consisting of one marriage or a larger church consisting of many marriages, we are designed to live in loving, authentic communities of equity providing a harmonious support for one another. This is a harvest worth laboring for.

CHAPTER 4

Marriage is a Church

Adam and Eve Go to Church

Adam and Eve were the first marriage and the first church. In the garden, they experienced the perfection of what marriage and church could be like.

After the fall, as the world became populated and infected with the devastating effects of sin, I can only imagine how much they missed their community with each other and their Creator.

How desperately they must have desired to replicate their garden days!

To do that, however, there would have been things they needed to know, do, and learn—and then teach these things to other members of their community who had not experienced garden life as they had.

They would want to know how to work together effectively and rule equitably together again, since the fall had messed everything up.

To be the power couple they were designed to be, they would want to know how they are made as humans to operate in their authentic goodness, rather than the desperate effects of sin. They would also want to know how to restore relationship with God, themselves, each other, and their now dying, ever-shifting earth.

I'm sure parenting would be a hot topic for them as their first child didn't turn out so well, forever marked as the first murderer.

They would be concerned for how to re-establish a close, talking relationship with God, their first friend and father.

They also would care about how to rule effectively and efficiently together since the fall. The fighting and bickering of who does what and who is better at what is getting exhausting as they miss their carefree harmonious garden days, where they effortlessly operated in equity together.

They would understand the effects of shame and desire to have a more honoring and loving relationship with themselves, as they strove to forgive themselves for their wretched error.

The last thing they would want to be reminded of is their terrible mistake and how to continually manage their fallen lives, with a how-to manual to live their new cursed existence.

Above all, I believe they would want to emulate a life that held the closest representation to the garden days as they could have. If they couldn't have their paradise back, they would want to know how to live this life with as much authenticity and similarities as their garden days with themselves and others.

I think they would have been the loudest celebrants to the ministry of Jesus had they lived long enough to see and experience him. I can just see them both hollering, "YEEESSSS!!! Garden days here we come!" They of all people knew what it was like to live in complete harmony and peace with one another, God, and the earth and then not have it. I believe they would have jumped at the opportunity to create a newly restored community that echoed their cherished garden days. They would want to be "that couple" again who ruled in power and equity. Or as I like to call them, the original models for Superman and Wonder Woman and the ultimate power couple.

Living the Real Thing

In my middle school in the mid-eighties, Lacoste polo shirts were very popular. If you're nodding nostalgically with a slight smile right now, you're my new best friend. To have the coveted little alligator on that supple cotton shirt was the envy of every middle schooler in my small private school in Bermuda Dunes, California.

Due to limited resources in our home, I had only one Lacoste polo, so I decided to make my own by cutting the alligator logo off a too-big polo shirt I found in a thrift shop and sewing it onto one of my plain polos. Every time I wore it, I was so terrified I would be discovered I couldn't even enjoy the counterfeit shirt.

Then one day, my worst fear came true. One of my classmates, suspicious of my shirt's authenticity, checked my shirt label while she sat behind me in class and discovered no Lacoste tag. She then considered it her personal duty to inform everyone else in the room of my shirt's inauthenticity. I was mortified and never attempted to counterfeit a Lacoste shirt again. To this day, if I wear a knock-off of a popular brand, I have no problem announcing its price or lack of authenticity. I decided it's better to be honest than to mislead.

There is nothing like the real thing. And if we attempt to mimic the real thing with a counterfeit, *we* will know the truth—and so will any keen observer. Then when you get found out, the embarrassment can be uncomfortable and difficult to explain.

Yet, great things are always imitated, and great people impersonated. It's called the Fakes Industry which makes $461 billion per year counterfeiting the latest fashion designers.[1] The popularity of social media speaks to how much people want to emulate their favorite humans as companies solicit "influencers" with trendy platforms to persuade others to buy their products. Patents have created a big industry to protect the genuine product from being illegally manufactured.

This is how I see marriages today.

We are so caught up in the latest counterfeit ideologies we are missing out on the real deal.

When women and men come together, we are designed to be a dynamic force that can reflect God's perfect image as we rule, subdue, and populate the earth—together, harmoniously and equitably. Whether in a marital or working relationship, we are designed organically and authentically to rule and partner equitably together. In the garden, there was no hierarchy, gender wars, abuse, or marginalization of either gender. Both man and woman reflected the image of a perfect being, and both were ordained to care for the earth harmoniously together.

Author Carolyn Custis James calls this synergy, the Blessed Alliance.[2] Since the fall, couples and marriages have evolved significantly, and today we see all sorts of marriages and couples. Doctrines and theologies have been developed to keep a patriarchal and hierarchal system in place, yet this was not the original or authentic design. We have developed a knock-off of the original and we wonder why we can't feel real love and connection with our spouses.

Called to Oneness

It is no coincidence that marriage and church are both called to oneness, or that God uses marriage analogies for describing his church, calling us "the bride of Christ."[3] If we are not living a loving relationship in our marriages, we are not able to live a loving relationship in our churches. Since God calls both institutions—church and marriage—to operate in oneness, love, and unity, patriarchalism and hierarchical principles are counter-scriptural and counter-culture for both.

Breaking the bonds of patriarchalism in religion so the feminine spirit can join collaboratively with the masculine spirit creates a dynamic, influential force. This is true regardless of your gender, since some people subscribe more to either the feminine or male spirit.

Renowned theorist and son of a preacher, Carl Jung "had a deep appreciation of our creative life and considered spirituality a central part of the human journey."[4] At one point, he aspired to be a pastor himself but turned to psychology to express his spiritual beliefs integrated with psychoanalysis.

He believed we need to embrace the femininity and masculinity within each of us to experience a full and meaningful life. In women, the male part was called the *animus* and in men the female part was called the *anima*.[5] Since both men and women are made in the image of God, it is no surprise we each have a masculine and feminine part regardless of our birth gender. When we can reconcile the masculinity and femininity in ourselves, this gives room for empathy and compassion to grow, thus diminishing judgements and division for one other.

As we represent the image of an awesome, dual-gendered, triune God, I compare it to Wonder Woman and Superman joining forces as they combine their superpowers to implement justice and look great doing it. They blow gender stereotypes out of the water as they operate according to their superpowers, abilities, and resources.

When they team up, they produce a dynamic force that inspires the weariest of souls to fight evil, save the underdog, and make the world a safer place.

At no time will you hear Superman saying to Wonder Woman, "You're inferior to me, so do what I say." That would mar their whole beautiful partnership. Nor will you hear Wonder Woman criticizing Superman for being weak because of the crippling effects of kryptonite. Or Superman criticizing Wonder Woman for being too masculine in her fights for justice. Superman will never say, "Give me your lasso. You throw like a girl."

You'll never hear either one of them attack the other's gender, strength, or capability. They rely, trust, and work passionately together to fight for justice and right the wrongs of the world.

A travesty occurs when we abandon that model and embrace a counterfeit relationship model where we fight and judge each other as we strive for positions of power and dominance. A tragic distortion happens when we dismiss the beautiful attributes of each gender residing in each of us. Like a king of the hill game gone awry, we do whatever it takes to stomp on those around us so they can be used to advance us to the top of the pile.

And when this happens, we miss out on the very heart of the authentic story to partner together equitably so we can accomplish the important task of managing this earth together.

What if we as men and women put our differences aside, silenced divisive beliefs, and worked to create alliances that supported and valued each individual? What if we worked to develop and accept the masculinity and femininity in ourselves? What could we accomplish as a church? In our marriages? Communities? Our world? If the church is offering a divisive culture for men and women based on gender roles, it is not offering a relevant support to modern marriages. This confuses and compromises marriages, preventing partners from being their best together so they can change our world for the better.

Responses to the patriarchal oppression throughout the years have been feminism, Affirmative Action, women's march, #metoo, #churchtoo, and other movements that have sparked national responses.

Although these are responses that address the symptoms of patriarchalism and a hierarchical system, we need to address the roots of patriarchalism and the hierarchical values that have negatively influenced—and continue to negatively influence—our Christian cultures.

In a nutshell, patriarchalism has had its time but is outdated for modern Western societies.

Where love in marriage used to be enough, now contemporary couples long for equality. To change a culture, we must create a new culture, speak a new language, and develop a new mindset that is inclusive and affirming of both genders to lead and live with excellence, authenticity, and integrity. We must believe that we are truly better together and that love transforms everything making all things new and improved.

Establishing a culture of gender parity in our attitudes, marriages, communities, and churches is essential for meeting the needs of modern marriages and to be culturally relevant to a society based on freedom and equality for all. Gaining a vision for gender parity is essential in moving forward in creating a better culture for marriages and churches to thrive in.

Marriages are mini-churches offering us an intimate glimpse of how we are called to sacrificially love one another with grace and equity, as we place God as the true head of the marriage. Operating as equals and valuing the differences each offers to complement the strength of the marriage also represents the one-body concept God calls his church to operate in. Oneness is practiced, not inherited, as individualist ideals are replaced with community values, and the two become one.

This matters because what we practice in our marriages becomes the central force to what we build in our church communities.

When marriages are misaligned, inequitable, unloving, and conflictive, the church body suffers in achieving oneness. Marriages teach us how to love, be kind, humble, live peaceably, be patient, and to live in unity. They become the sanctuaries in which we experience love, enabling us to unapologetically develop all the femininity and masculinity within each of us. Marriage inspires character development and teaches us how to love unconditionally.

Churches and spiritual communities need to support modern marriages in their relationship development so we can create a place of hope, harmony, and equity, fueled by love and grace, and grounded in truth.

William Keepin, author of *Divine Duality*, gives a beautiful vision of how we can work together to create garden living by "building an altogether new level of integrity and harmony between women and men that will one day enable humanity to reclaim the magic of balanced communion between masculine and feminine."[6]

Ahhh yes, the magic of the garden days.

It may not be as far out of reach as we imagine.

In the next chapter, let's explore a popular marriage model in America today called Peer Marriages.

CHAPTER 5

Becoming Peer

Peer Marriage

Jill and Rylie had been married for over ten years, and both had full-time jobs.

Before they had kids, they split the household chores according to what they liked doing. Rylie loved doing laundry, while Jill enjoyed mowing the grass. Rylie relished cooking, while Jill was skilled at accounting and managing the family finances. Even though neither particularly enjoyed cleaning, they split the household chores fairly.

When kids came along, Jill and Rylie struggled to keep up with their jobs, do household chores, and parent effectively. They were worn out.

Instead of one person picking up the slack, they both sat down and discussed what they each wanted to do to make the kid transition easier for both. They decided to do the chores they enjoyed, then bring in a housekeeper twice a month to clean their house. Then they split up watching and caring for the kids, one parent taking charge of baths, the other parent getting kids into bed, one helping with homework, the other in change of taxiing children to activities.

They took turns taking time away from family responsibilities to invest in themselves. They both contributed to setting up date nights, as one would get the sitter and the other plan the date. When they had conflict, they both agreed to fair fighting rules, and when they were hurtful, they each would make amends.

Perfection was never the goal as much as developing a healthy partnership. As parenting demands grew, Jill and Rylie negotiated what each could provide, hired help as needed, and partnered together to make the home run smoothly while supporting each other in their advancing careers.

Their marriage was flexible and grew with the demands of the home, kids, and work as each partnered together to pick up the growing load while being responsible for the capacity of their own load.

Rylie and Jill are a great example of a Peer Marriage.

What is a Peer Marriage?

I love this definition from Ruth Haley Barton: "A marriage that works frees both the wife and the husband (partners) to continue to discover who they are and to function as a team according to their gifts, personalities and strengths."[1]

Before the fall, Adam and Eve had a Peer Marriage.

Many couples today are already pursuing this kind of marriage. Due to the growth of women in the US workforce, the majority of couples subscribe to egalitarian values, parenting and providing together. In fact, 72 percent of millennials consider this their ideal relationship.

University of Washington professor Dr. Pepper Schwartz calls these "Peer Marriages," which are in sharp contrast to the patriarchal model once popularly held by marriages. These marriages are egalitarian in that ". . . couples have successfully reconstructed gender roles on a genuinely equitable basis."[2]

Another name for this emerging relationship style is relational reciprocity. These are marriages where couples ". . . make continued efforts to demonstrate care in terms of looking out for each other, communicating about each other's thoughts and opinions, and an overall commitment to the longevity of the relationship despite all odds."[3]

In other words, these marriages reflect a connected companionship comprised of equality, value, and deep friendship.

Relational reciprocity is built as tasks are shared and a partnership, rather than a hierarchical relationship, is emphasized. Flexibility is a key component to establishing equality in these relationships, as ongoing negotiations are necessary in order to navigate the needs and expectations of both partners.

Peer Marriages mirror the original design of marriage, because God designed men and women to rule together: in Genesis, God commanded men and women to rule over all he had created—and to do it together.

There is a shared balance of power as Peer Marriages experience a "power with" instead of a "power over" as they partner and lead together to grow and stabilize their marriage.

Here are some interesting statistics related to Peer Marriages:

- Peer Marriages recognize a decrease in marital conflict, divisive issues, and lower likelihood of divorce.[4]
- Women in peer marriages claim greater happiness, more stability, health, open communication, and greater sexual satisfaction.[5]
- Men describe a value of being more relational and have a greater understanding of maintaining a healthy relational connection.[6]

Couples are coming up with a new solution to cultural changes and learning to overcome the negative effects of their ejection from the garden.

They are learning a new culture, a new language, and mirroring the spiritual values of healthy community. They are learning to live in love, share the labor responsibilities, and come together in working equitably with one another. They are capitalizing on their similarities, diminishing their differences, and embracing a new way of living that brings hope, life, and fulfillment.

Despite the challenges and different models of their families of origin, they are learning to speak the language of love, full of grace, acceptance, and partnership. This is reflecting the authentic, original design creating oneness through respect, equity, peace, and love. They reign like kings and queens in their kingdom as they speak a regal language befitting of two equally powerful rulers.

Near Peer Marriages

Many couples strive to design contemporary relational models, such as the Peer Marriage model but wrestle with the implementation process.[7] Despite their obvious strengths, Peer Marriages do exhibit some challenges and weaknesses:

- Partners in Near Peer Marriages struggle with not having a map or "blueprint" for their contemporary marriage and often wonder if they are doing marriage correctly.
- Because they lack an understanding of the design for their egalitarian marriage, they create it as they go along.
- There can be confusion and power struggles for control and getting needs met if the couple's negotiation skills are underdeveloped or undisclosed gender stereotypes emotionally hijack the partnership.

Unfortunately, even within couples longing for gender parity, outdated narratives can continue to have an influence, causing partners to eventually gravitate back to society's values instead of pushing through to embrace characteristics that help them connect fairly with the opposite gender.

These struggling marriages, often in a perpetually conflictive and confused state, have been described as "Near Peer" by author and professor Dr. Pepper Schwartz.[8]

Near Peer describes couples that hold egalitarian values and beliefs, but struggle to operate in these behaviors in practice.

Even when couples agree to egalitarian principles, studies show they have challenges practicing equality, and that they hold conflicting beliefs regarding gender roles. And sometimes a relationship that began successfully as a Peer Marriage evolves into a Near Peer Marriage when there is a job change or the family structure changes with the introduction of kids.

In a Near Peer Marriage, couples may exhibit low deference to each other, making the man's career the top priority, and following gender-stereotypical roles in the home. Conflict resolution can consist of passive aggressive and manipulative behaviors instead of negotiation and compromising strategies.

As you can imagine, this creates conflict and confusion for the couple, as they say one thing but do another, becoming trapped in perpetual power struggles. Hierarchical values and a fear of loss of power undermine the marital partnership, as each partner vies for control. Progress becomes challenging if not impossible as energy is relegated to establishing control in the relationship instead of developing a healthy connection.

What does this look like in real life?

Todd and Stacy considered themselves equal partners who both worked full-time jobs and helped care for the kids.

Yet, when Stacy came home from her long day of teaching, she found herself cooking meals, cleaning the house, and caring for the kids, while Todd watched golf, worked on the computer, or read the paper.

When she asked him for help with the household chores, he agreed to be fair and split the work, except he just didn't do it no matter what Stacy did to motivate him to do his part. She made chore charts, explained her need for help, complained, pleaded, and became angry, but Todd would do just enough to keep her happy then revert to doing whatever he wanted.

When she asked him to fix meals, he complained that he didn't know how to cook and would be too busy to make dinner, or he would make the same meal every time. Their intimacy life revolved primarily around Todd's desires even though Stacy repeatedly requested more effort and consideration from him in meeting her sexual needs.

When it came to watching the kids, he refused to follow the education plans or chore plans Stacy set up for the kids, and often got lost working on the computer, golfing, or frequently working late at the office. When Stacy asked for help with the yard, garage, or fixing things around the house, Todd would agree to do it but often not follow through, then get mad when she tried to hold him accountable.

Finally, Stacy became so frustrated she hired extra household help, which irritated Todd. This led to perpetual conflicts, and ultimately the trust and good will became broken because Todd pretended to have a Peer Marriage, but showed no accountability or responsibility in his partnership with Stacy. He failed to see how his manipulation and passive-aggressive behavior hurt trust with her and caused her to depend on others for partnership.

Todd's broken promises of equity and partnership with Stacy caused her chronic disappointment, broke her trust, and placed her in a double bind with Todd. She couldn't win by talking, planning, or complaining to him, because Todd would just do what he wanted. And she couldn't win by doing everything herself because she was exhausted and worn out from her work.

Todd liked to describe his relationship as a Peer Marriage where he treated his wife with equity, but in reality, his unrealistic partner expectations of Stacy became a classic and familiar example of a Near Peer Marriage. Saying one thing but doing another creates instability in any environment.

Moving from Near Peer to Peer

Marriages can function for a long time in this frustrating Near Peer status—especially when they don't have any other vision for operating differently.

But making the shift to—or back to—a Peer Marriage doesn't have to feel like rocket science, particularly as couples grasp the vision and begin to practice key skills that make it possible.

Take, for example, the experience of Max and Sandra.

Max and Sandra were operating in a Near Peer Marriage. Even though they both were called to pastor a church plant, Max was the designated Lead Pastor, and Sandra continued her teaching position, parenting their children, and assisting Max.

Both became overwhelmed trying to pursue their ministry calling while also providing for their family, and the strain of their Catch-22 became evident.

A church leader who noticed their predicament suggested a Peer Marriage model where they could both pursue their pastoral calling, parent, and both provide financially for their family.

This new vision included Max co-pastoring with Sandra, increasing his parenting time, and overcoming stereotypes of being the solo lead of their family.

It also included Sandra quitting her teaching job to co-pastor with Max, sharing parenting time, and overcoming stereotypes preventing her from being a female pastor.

After weighing the pros and cons, Max and Sandra abandoned their Near Peer Marriage and began the pursuit of a true Peer Marriage model, mutually operating as co-pastors and co-parents.

They both had desired the value of equally contributing to the marriage and family, but neither had the vision or strategy to develop what they longed to experience. When a vision and strategies were proposed to them, they successfully achieved their dream.

A Milestone in Our Movement from Near Peer to Peer

Jake and I had to grow into a Peer Marriage ourselves, and one of the areas we struggled with was how to share feedback with each other without reacting defensively or feeling attacked.

It's easy to love each other and express acceptance when we're pleasing each other but when we are frustrating each other, this becomes more challenging. Jake and I realized we both can get bent out of shape when we perceive that we are being criticized. This can raise defenses and create a fight instead of fostering an environment where we can meet each other's needs.

One of the techniques we learned that helped us tremendously was borrowed from Jack Canfield's *Secret of Success* book. The technique is simply to thank people for their feedback no matter how they offer it.

I shared this strategy with Jake during one of our vacations.

Later in the day I told him I felt he wasn't listening to me when I was talking to him, paying attention instead to his phone or watch, looking over my head, and giving a half-hearted answer.

He started to react defensively, then he took a deep breath, softened his face, looked me straight in the eyes and said, "Thank you for the feedback."

Wow.

I've never felt more loved and valued than I did in that moment.

There's no question that respect, equity, affirmation, and love are arts that we will spend our entire lives and marriages learning. But the point is that we have to keep learning.

Jake and I are still perfecting what it looks like to work with unity and equity and operate as co-rulers of two very different kingdoms, and as we work with other couples, we have developed a word picture that often helps couples on their own journey.

Let me tell you the story of Shelly and Pete.

Shelly and Pete came to see me, and both were yelling at the same time to be heard in my office. Pete blamed Shelly's outrageous anger on menopause, and Shelly blamed Pete for years of ignoring her and spending all his spare time hunting.

To stop the perpetual fighting, I asked a question I often ask of couples. "Who in your relationship holds the most power?"

Predictably, Pete and Shelly pointed to each other.

I looked at Pete and said, "You are the king of your kingdom."

He nodded smugly at Shelly as if to say, *Look, she's on my side.*

"And it's the blue kingdom," I continued before turning to Shelly. "And you're the queen of the pink kingdom."

Then I addressed them both. "Pete, you are not the king of pink kingdom, and Shelly, you are not the queen of blue kingdom. But you are co-rulers of the purple kingdom. You both must come together as king and queen to rule the kingdom that lies between the two of you and consists fully of each of you. Stop trying to rule each other's kingdom, and start taking full responsibility for ruling your own kingdom so you can be effective in ruling together."

What I described to Pete and Shelly is the picture of a "power couple" where each partner is ruling with his or her full strength and power to create a mutual kingdom in which both partners can thrive.

As Pete and Shelly began operating in this mode, they stopped yelling to be heard because power was reinstated to each of them. People who rage, yell, and scream to be heard are almost always operating out of fear—and, indeed, both Pete and Shelly had been terrified of losing power. They didn't want the pain of being rejected and ignored, and they didn't want the pain of being bullied and dismissed.

But when we accept the idea that we can't rule a partner's kingdom and may or may not even be able to create a purple kingdom together—but we are always the rulers of our personal kingdoms—that fear subsides. No one can take power away from us unless we let them. We always have the power to choose how to respond instead of reacting to whatever is delivered to us.

Author and professor Ruth Haley Barton describes the beauty of marriage and what we all long for: "Two individuals love and give to each other in such a way that both souls are nourished. A husband commits himself to love, nurture and see that his wife has what she needs to be all that she is meant to be—to the point of laying down his own comfort, indeed his very life. The wife gives to her husband out of the fullness that comes from being truly loved and nurtured into full personhood. Their balance and unity speak volumes to a world burdened with trying to find love in relationships fraught with domination, manipulation, power struggles and selfishness."[9]

This is what I like to call "making purple" and learning to rule the "purple kingdom" as kings and queens. We do all that we can to make harmony and unity together so we can be better together and make this world a better place.

The pink/blue kingdom is a helpful example for people in heterosexual Peer Marriages often struggling to appreciate the unique differences in each gender represented.

Examples like this can help shift perspectives and even paradigms.

But the other element that is foundational for a couple to grow into a true Peer Marriage is character development.

The fact is that mature and improved character development creates mature marriages. When we grow our character, our relationships also grow.

Character growth improves upon the God-given personality you have as a unique individual. When we have poor character or refuse to grow and mature our character, we can behave like selfish, rude children who have never been taught to live with courtesy, generosity, or self-restraint.

As humans, we are called to grow up and develop character to complement our unique personalities: "When I was a child, I talked like a child, I thought like a child, I reasoned like a child. When I became a man, I put the ways of childhood behind me" (1 Corinthians 13:11).

Character development is so crucial, we'll be taking a deeper look at it in a later section. But I will leave you with this for now: When we seek to develop the God-piece in all of us, we are able to divinely breathe life through our relationships and accentuate the best in each of us.

Peer Marriage Assessment

Is the marriage you have a true Peer Marriage or a Near Peer Marriage? The following assessment can help you determine the answer to this question.

Peer/Near Peer Marriage Assessment

1. ☐ Yes ☐ No   Do you both hold equal
                    leadership positions in the
                    marriage?

2. ☐ Yes ☐ No   Do you both get equal talk
                    time in sharing, conflicts, and
                    social outings?

3. ☐ Yes ☐ No   Are you both considered
                    equal contributors even if one
                    partner is the financial provider
                    and one the household or
                    childcare provider?

4. ☐ Yes ☐ No   Do you both have equal
                  decision power for purchases,
                  and saving or spending the
                  money?

5. ☐ Yes ☐ No   Do you both accept the
                  influence of the other in the
                  areas in which each is skilled,
                  i.e., relationships, finances,
                  parenting?

6. ☐ Yes ☐ No   Are you both able to give leadership
                  influence and partner in all areas
                  regardless of gender stereotypes and
                  expectations?

7. ☐ Yes ☐ No   Do you feel the freedom to lead, and be
                  respected and followed by your partner?

8. ☐ Yes ☐ No   Are you careful about not using gender-
                  division stereotypes, i.e., women can't
                  drive well, men who cry are weak?

9. ☐ Yes ☐ No   Do you celebrate both female and male
                  leaders, authors, artists?

10. ☐ Yes ☐ No   Are you both supportive of each
                  furthering your education or careers?

11. ☐ Yes ☐ No   Are your sons, daughters, nieces, and
                  nephews both promoted to be qualified
                  leaders according to ability and not
                  gender?

12. ☐ Yes ☐ No   Do each of you follow female/
male leadership in the home and outside
of the home respectfully, without
eyerolling, mocking, or undermining
humor that marginalizes or invalidates
the wife/mom in the home?

13. ☐ Yes ☐ No   Are you respectful and supportive of one
another according to your gifts and
abilities even if those abilities are
counter to gender stereotypes?

14. ☐ Yes ☐ No   Is the wife pursued and validated for
what she can offer in her leadership
ability?

15. ☐ Yes ☐ No   Are there equal advancement
opportunities for both of you to excel
in whatever you are interested in?

16. ☐ Yes ☐ No   Does your marriage claim values of
equity and reflect this in daily living?

17. ☐ Yes ☐ No   Are both followed and promoted as
spiritual leaders in the home?

18. ☐ Yes ☐ No   In social settings, are women part of
gender-inclusive conversations
where they can participate because they
have a shared knowledge of the topic
(i.e., sports stats or sports analogies)?

19. ☐Yes ☐No   In social settings, are men part of gender-inclusive conversations where they can participate because they have a shared knowledge of the topic (i.e., hair and beauty tips)?

20. ☐Yes ☐No   Do you both show respect with eye contact when speaking and offer affirmation for expressed opinions and thoughts?

21. ☐Yes ☐No   Do you introduce your partner in social settings?

22. ☐Yes ☐No   Do you share household and parenting responsibilities?

23. ☐Yes ☐No   Do you have an equal division of labor that you are both comfortable with?

24. ☐Yes ☐No   When the husband/wife or other men/women use sarcasm, stereotypes, or objectifying humor to marginalize and invalidate male/female leaders, are they corrected?

25. ☐Yes ☐No   Does each of you express your boundaries and respect each other's boundaries?

26. ☐Yes ☐No   Do you each express feelings and needs to your partner?

27. ☐ Yes ☐ No   Do each of you express a need for the
                  other to partner with him/her?

28. ☐ Yes ☐ No   Are there appropriate relationships with
                  the opposite gender outside of marriage
                  that both of you are comfortable with?

29. ☐ Yes ☐ No   Is there a security in the marriage that
                  each will behave appropriately with the
                  opposite gender?

30. ☐ Yes ☐ No   If there has been infidelity or
                  inappropriateness in the marriage, has
                  the offender made appropriate amends?

31. ☐ Yes ☐ No   Is there a concern expressed by each
                  of you to make it right if one or both
                  are feeling disrespected, marginalized,
                  unheard, or mistreated in the marriage?

32. ☐ Yes ☐ No   When each of you asks to be
                  comforted, protected, or connected
                  with, does each receive this consistently?

33. ☐ Yes ☐ No   Do you both laugh, applaud, and
                  celebrate one another when it is
                  deserved?

34. ☐ Yes ☐ No   Do you both comfort, and express
                  empathy and care, when there has been
                  a loss or a crisis?

35. ☐ Yes ☐ No   Do you each utilize marriage books,
                  resources, and counseling that reflect
                  egalitarian values?

36. ☐ Yes ☐ No Does the marriage culture provide freedom and support for each of you to be who you need to be?

37. ☐ Yes ☐ No Do both of you feel like God reflects your femininity as a woman and your masculinity as a man?

38. ☐ Yes ☐ No Are both men and women honored in your family history through pictures, stories, and visits?

39. ☐ Yes ☐ No Do you follow through with what you promise privately and act as promised publicly, (i.e., promise to refrain from hurtful teasing and act accordingly in public)?

40. ☐ Yes ☐ No Do both of you apologize for unfair treatment and make amends by creating equity, justice, and psychological safety for each of you?

41. ☐ Yes ☐ No If there are opportunities for the husband/wife to mentor the opposite gender outside of the marriage, is it done appropriately or to the comfort of each of you?

42. ☐ Yes ☐ No Do you both feel free to express your opinions, advocate for equitable treatment, and receive the care and help from the other to get your needs met?

43. ☐ Yes ☐ No   Are wives empowered to advocate for
other women leaders and girls without
being negatively labeled or blocked by
the husband?

44. ☐ Yes ☐ No   Are you both held personally
accountable for immoral or disrespectful
behavior that hurts the marriage?

45. ☐ Yes ☐ No   Are there ongoing marriage classes or
resources implemented that might
promote gender parity in the marriage
(i.e., defining emotional manipulation,
unfair fighting)?

46. ☐ Yes ☐ No   Is there an expressed value in words and
actions by both of you for equity in
the marriage?

47. ☐ Yes ☐ No   Are there productive discussions on how
to be better together and more loving
partners?

48. ☐ Yes ☐ No   Are each of you credited publicly and
privately for your ideas, solutions, and
contributions?

49. ☐ Yes ☐ No   Are you both respectful of each
other's voice by not interrupting during
conflicts, discussions, socializing, or
playful banter?

50. ☐ Yes ☐ No When working outside of the home is gender-balanced leadership desired?

51. ☐ Yes ☐ No When there is an issue for one, do both of you approach one another to receive support and understanding?

52. ☐ Yes ☐ No In family activities, are women acknowledged in social interactions the same as men and vice versa?

53. ☐ Yes ☐ No Do you both express gratitude and appreciation for each other's perspectives and differences?

54. ☐ Yes ☐ No When women speak, are they heard, helped, and honored for what they feel and need without ridicule for being needy?

55. ☐ Yes ☐ No When men speak, are they heard, helped, and honored for what they feel and need without ridicule for being weak?

56. ☐ Yes ☐ No Do you both take turns partnering and caring for the children?

57. ☐ Yes ☐ No If it is a dual income home, are both careers considered equally valuable thus making childcare a shared responsibility in order for both partners to further their careers?

58. ☐ Yes ☐ No   Do you both create flexibility in your schedules as much as possible to allow the other to pursue their life, education, or career goals?

59. ☐ Yes ☐ No   Is there equal free time and personal recreation time for each of you?

60. ☐ Yes ☐ No   Do you both have equal access to finances and input on financial goals?

61. ☐ Yes ☐ No   Are roles assigned by giftedness instead of gender within the marriage and home?

62. ☐ Yes ☐ No   Is there a strong friendship in the marriage?

63. ☐ Yes ☐ No   Do you both believe you have a mutually satisfying sex life?

64. ☐ Yes ☐ No   Are both of you free to pursue sexual connection with your partner?

65. ☐ Yes ☐ No   Do you feel emotionally connected to your partner?

66. ☐ Yes ☐ No   Do you feel known by your partner?

67. ☐ Yes ☐ No   Do you feel like you matter and are valued by your partner?

68. ☐ Yes ☐ No   Are you both filling out this assessment?

Scoring:

If you answered 50-68 questions with "no" then this is a Non-Peer Marriage.

If you answered 20-49 of the questions with "no" then this is considered a Near Peer Marriage.

If you answered 19 or fewer of the questions with "no" then this is a Peer Marriage.

CHAPTER 6

The Impact of the Fall on Churches

As we've been examining, it's no easy task to develop the coveted Peer Marriage. But couples *are* succeeding. And if marriages can do it, so can churches.

Of course, the posture of too many churches (and the experience of too many men and women) tell us we have far to go.

Since the fall when we disobeyed God, we have been separated from him and each other. Consumed with dominance teaching and the posturing of men over women, men have been designated as the primary spiritual directors, thus sidelining women from partnering with men in church leadership.

The Liturgists Podcast emphasized that if the church selects leadership according to genital parts and limits them in their roles, it is a "dehumanization of women" and it is "anti-Christ" for the church.[1]

The marginalization of women is causing much hurt in our marriages, relationships, and churches today. This has created what psychologists are identifying as a deep psychological grief from the profound loss of women leaders and pastors within the church. This is a synthetic or counterfeit model for the genders, and spiritual communities are a far cry from the original, authentic design. (A fake Lacoste shirt comes to mind. . .)

How did we get here?

A Tragic Narrative

Humans decided to take things in their own hands and discover for themselves who and what they were designed for. Adam and Eve disobeyed God, ate the forbidden fruit, and their eyes were opened to good and evil and shame of their nakedness. In their shame, they attempted to cover themselves, and the curse of their actions led to difficult, painful labor in farming and in childbearing.

This is where we see blame, division, and hierarchy come in as man is placed over woman, and Adam blames Eve for eating the fruit. A new BS (blame and shame) culture is created with a new damning language spoken called D3—deception, dominance, and division—and the perfect, beautiful garden becomes a poor fit for their imperfect culture.

With the death of the authentic Adam and Eve, so too came the death of what was, as the original Adam and Eve became replaced with a synthetic version of themselves and were banished outside of the garden. They are separated from the goodness of the garden, the innocence of perfect love, and from their best friend and Creator.

"It is not good for the man to be alone." (Genesis 2:18)

Men and women forget we need each other. But the further we get from garden living, the more inequities and hierarchies mar the garden life.

According to shame expert Brené Brown, "Shaming and blaming without accountability is toxic to couples, families, organizations, and communities."[2]

We weren't designed to live in this type of BS environment as it is not the original habitat for humans. The D3 language is damning us to an out-of-garden existence.

Here's how this is playing out in our culture and churches today: abuse and sexism, creating a separation, loss, and deep sadness. Fear has replaced love, and survival of the fittest has become the new norm.

One of the greatest ambassadors of this counterfeit tragic narrative is patriarchalism.

Six Reasons Patriarchalism Doesn't Work Today

Patriarchalism is a result of living outside the garden. It defies the very creation design and goes against garden living. When God said it wasn't good for man to be alone, and man decided it was good for man to be alone, we were once again participating in the disobedience of the fall.

Patriarchalism is an ineffective and culturally delayed leadership style for Western culture and contemporary marriages. From my studies, I discovered that it is counter-cultural to Christianity, profanes the image of God, misuses Scripture, has a negative impact on churches and marriages, reinforces gender stereotypes, and provokes a profound loss for the church.

Let's take a look at each of these.

1. Patriarchalism is Counter-Cultural to Christianity

Patriarchalism is counter-cultural to Christianity as evidenced through scripture and the ministry of Jesus.

In Genesis, a marriage command is given: "For this reason a man will leave his father and mother and be united to his wife and they will become one flesh" (Genesis 2:24).

Eventually patriarchalism would demand that a woman, as property, leave her family and become a part of the man's family.[3]

But God's original intent cannot be ignored. He commanded the man to leave his family and unite harmoniously with his wife.

In addition, God repeatedly goes against the patriarchal culture in the Old Testament by passing over the eldest son in favor of giving a blessing to the youngest time and again. Jacob received the blessing instead of his elder brother Esau. Joseph's youngest son Ephraim was blessed instead of Manasseh. David was the youngest, yet he was anointed as king, and so on.[4] In this way, God repeatedly opposes the patriarchal culture of biblical days, thereby releasing women from the bonds of patriarchalism.

Does this hold true in the New Testament as well?

Absolutely.

In the New Testament, Jesus' association with women dramatically denounces the patriarchal culture when he acknowledges women as ministry partners. He converses with women, eats with them, and heals them in an era where this was culturally taboo.

In addition, the early Acts church repelled patriarchal culture when women worshiped together with men and became teachers, apostles, and evangelists of the faith. To disregard women as equal partners in marriage or church in favor of a hierarchical culture, as introduced through the fall, is to disregard the culture of Christ and the freedom he died to bring.

2. Patriarchalism Profanes the Image of God

Since men and women were both created in the image of God, to exalt one over the other is to misrepresent and profane the very image of God.[5]

Both were created to represent his image, therefore, neither should be considered more valuable than the other. Each gender is uniquely created and necessary in the institutions of marriage and the church to better understand the intricate nature and character of God.

When women are silenced through patriarchalism, men are impoverished, having lost the opportunity to experience the nurturing, mothering part of God. In the words of Carolyn Custis James, we are to partner together so as "to beam back to heaven the clearest and fullest images of (God) himself."[6]

3. Patriarchalism Misuses Scripture

Misunderstandings of controversial scripture have supported patriarchalism in our marriages and in the church. Scriptures such as "for the husband is the head of the wife as Christ is the head of the church" (Ephesians 5:23) or "Women should remain silent in the churches" (1Corinthians 14:34) and are forbidden to teach men (1 Timothy 2:11–12) have been misused and misinterpreted.

They are supporting texts electing patriarchalism to be the divine order in marriages and in church, complete with creative descriptions of what it culturally means to be the "head" of the home.

Instead of considering the spirit of the gospel, these disputed scriptures have divided Christians worldwide, leading them to operate with the drive to dominate in a fallen state of fear, shame, and separation, versus living in mutuality with love, grace and unity as prescribed by God: "The redeemed desire is to love in mutuality."[7]

Patriarchalism appears to be in direct opposition to redemptive living and provokes conflict instead of positive connection in our marriages and churches.

4. Patriarchalism Negatively Impacts the Church

Similarly, where patriarchalism is in full bloom, half the church suffers as only half of the church is empowered to fully participate. Men lose their strong equal of women who are here to partner and empower them to finish this race well, together. For when patriarchalism reigns, women's voices are silenced as the male voice and presence take precedence. Men diminish their own power and potential as they lose the unique partnership women offer, and the magic of a gender synergy is lost.

When men are exalted at the cost of women, this also creates a breeding ground for gender inequality, grounds for infidelity or moral failings, abuse, and objectification of women. Abuse and violence are more common in patriarchal marriages, as women are expected to meet the needs and desires of their husbands without expressing resistance.

In addition, when moral failings happen in church leadership, church communities experience the relational loss as the moral errors are minimized and wives are encouraged to overlook or have compassion for their husband's infidelity. While women are called to reconcile through forgiveness, grace, and love, men are called to be accountable to God exclusively, rather than their wives as well.

This creates a lack of accountability and balance in the marriage and church community. When women are minimized and their main expected role is to complement their husbands in marriage or male leadership in the church, both institutions are deprived of women's relational giftedness, and all suffer.

In fact, families and couples suffer, too. Because for women to mediate the psychological tension of discrimination and sexism they use self-silencing behaviors, as they mute their own voices. In the process, relationships suffer as the relational strengths of connection, nurturance, and intimacy are withdrawn. Indeed, women's unique ability to be guardians of relationships and attuned to emotional or physical distress and needs is diminished, thus exposing relationships to hardships and even burnout.

The point is that men lose in their marriages and families as well, because relational and emotional health is compromised when women are minimized and invalidated. When the health of marriages is compromised, church health is also negatively affected as both institutions miss out on the powerful female nurturing influence on relationships.

Patriarchalism inaccurately persuades and brainwashes men to believe they are benefiting from the male dominant culture when in truth men, along with women, are victims of it.

This misconception presents one of the greatest barriers in encouraging men to abandon patriarchalism.

5. Patriarchalism Propagates Stereotypes

Patriarchalism has been gravely misunderstood to benefit men when in reality both genders are emotionally and psychologically crippled when they act in the constraints of rigid stereotypes.[8] The genders are divided from operating together in a powerful, divine partnership, and society mourns the loss.

Throughout the ages, male aggressiveness has been promoted as ultimate masculinity and is admired by both genders. Ambitious, aggressive, driven men are heralded for being manly, strong warriors for communities, and coveted partners for women who historically depended on these traits for their survival.[9] Socially acceptable traits like arrogance, toughness, and aggressiveness are adopted by boys to cover less socially acceptable feelings of loneliness, powerlessness, and fear. Experts dubbed this the "boy code," allowing boys to remain safe behind a mask, a tough exterior to avoid taunting and rejection from society and peers for expressing vulnerable emotions.[10]

Tragically, when this happens, they are robbed of the ability to develop emotional intelligence, and they become skilled at disconnecting from their emotions and others.

While girls are accepted for expressing vulnerable emotions, like fear, helplessness, and pain, boys are stifled. This gap is dramatically displayed in marriage, ushering in grounds for a patriarchal relationship, where the emotionally crippled man denies emotions in himself and his wife.

Hiding his true self, the man finds more security and comfort in relying on a hierarchical system that will protect him from expressing his vulnerable emotions, keeping him in control. Commonly, men become "shame-phobic"[11] and will go to great lengths to avoid shame by choosing defensiveness to cover their vulnerability.

Shutting themselves off to others, men miss out on authentic relationships and community with women and society.

6. Patriarchalism Provokes a Psychological Sadness in the Body

The dismissal and silencing of women creates a gaping hole in the infrastructure of the church, provoking a sorrowful loss for the church body. Described by psychologists as the psychodynamics of sadness, this has a profound effect in every aspect of church culture and spiritual community as relationships are stifled and undeveloped.

Like the phantom pains experienced from a person's severed limb, so too the church body experiences pain from the severance of women's leadership. This is not how we were designed to operate as men and women in the body of Christ. David Westlake, author of *Why Gender Equality Matters*, bemoans this tragedy with his words:

"In the beginning God made men and women. Both were equally an expression of his image, character and love. Men and women were commissioned together for both child-rearing and ruling. Then the fall happened and what was meant to be together got broken. The world has been crying ever since."[12]

Understanding the various aspects of loss can help us dry up our tears and course correct so we can create a full and balanced community.

Four types of relational losses have been identified that are negatively impacting the church with the absence of women leaders:

1) *Intrapsychic loss*, where one loses what could have been as dreams are dashed

2) *Functional loss*, when an organization loses its functions as it struggles to operate with effectiveness and efficiency

3) *Role loss*, where a specific role is lost within a system

4) *System loss*, where one is no longer a part of the bigger system, as they are eliminated or operating on the fringe

In the loss of women church leaders, there is an undeniable aching sadness in many churches today. One church researcher states, "Loss is pervasive in the church and one can argue that the Protestant church in North America is a sad church, filled with loss and mourning."[13] With the significant gender gap in church leadership, the American church is missing the relational wealth women leaders offer alongside men. When they are silenced, excluded, and marginalized, psychological sadness fills the aching gap as men become the coveted, pursued leaders.

When Dr. Cho, pastor of the largest church in the world in Seoul, Korea, was weary and struggling to build his church, he discovered a solution that he readily offers to those seeking his advice: "Release your women."[14]

Yet, he often finds American pastors to be resistant to using this advice as a viable solution to building church membership.[15] Whether in marriage or church, the loss of the relational skills that women provide is having a grievous relational and emotional impact on the ethos of the church that few are identifying or problem-solving.

President of Fuller Theological Seminary Mark Labberton speaks to this sadness of the loss of women leaders in the church as the "groaning beauty" and questions how the church can deal with this gender abuse that is a "huge sorrow and groaning" for the church.[16] If this sadness is to be soothed, it appears more programs are not the solution, but rather the presence and influence of women leaders leading with men.

We can do better, and we must do better for this generation of marriages and the marriages in the generations to come. With some repentance, remodeling, and restructuring, I believe we can become whole and healthy and operate as we are designed to be: one body, full of life, health, and unity with diversity. Women are life-givers, created to give and nurture life, literally and symbolically, and their influence and leadership are a critical piece to giving relational life to a community and aiding in its transformation. Men plant the seeds for women to birth new life and harvest a beautiful crop. We need each other, every part, to operate with health and wholeness.

We were created to operate with diversity and unity, and the church is one of life's stages on which we waltz, jitterbug, and tango a dance harmoniously and rhythmically together.

When we ignore, mistreat, or misuse any part of our body, the dance becomes a painful, awkward, and uncomfortable experience for the viewer and the participants, as the dance competes uncomfortably with the music.

Individually and corporately, we have a responsibility to keep our bodies healthy and in good working condition so we can dance the purposed life we are passionate about living as a community. Just as our bodies become impaired or weakened when we overuse one part and underuse another, so too the community becomes weakened. When we rely too heavily on one part and dismiss or misuse others, it compromises the health of the whole body. We can become inflamed or swollen as a reminder to take care and show caution to the injured part, allowing a healing process as we rely on other parts to compensate for the healing time.

CHAPTER 7

Women and Church Culture

So what exactly is stopping women from being included in church culture with the same respect and equity as men?

In order to answer this, we need to understand the cultural and historical relationship of church and women, both currently and in past eras.

Hard Facts about Women and the Church

Research reveals that women are struggling to be treated with equity and professional respect within the church.

Like a wounded body, the American church body is showing signs of impairment and injury when it comes to establishing unity, specifically among the genders and with men and women leading together.

Masked patriarchy is covertly eliminating the women's influence in egalitarian church bodies as women are relegated to gender-specific roles, neglected with mentoring and restricted from preaching. When we diminish our women leaders, we dull our communities as relationships, nurturance, collaborative leadership, innovative programming, and creative design become just a few of the elements the church fails to experience. As a body, we are becoming swollen and agitated when we are not involving all the parts of our body, and infection is showing up in areas of abuse of women and children, moral failings, and the break-up of the family.

Shelia loved church and was grateful for the profound impact her church had on her life and that of her family. So it was no surprise she went to college to receive her ministry degree and was later hired at her hometown church to be a youth minister.

Although she was taught with equity alongside her male peers at her Christian university, she was never warned about the inequities she would endure in the church culture due to her gender.

In tears, she called me one day shocked about the inconsistencies she was experiencing as a woman minister in her church. She was paid less than her male colleagues yet doing the same position, was restricted from preaching even though the male pastors were encouraged to preach, and was not given opportunity for leadership advancement, unlike her male colleagues. When she questioned the head pastor about the inconsistencies and discrimination, she was pointed to scriptures preventing her from being a leader of equity within church. She was not allowed to preach, and instructed to be more submissive and to express gratitude that she was allowed to be a pastor at all!

Sadly, this is a very familiar story of women leaders in many leading churches today.

George Barna reports the overwhelming evidence of gender bias in the church: 97 percent of all senior pastors in the US are men. Women earn $5,000 per year less than male colleagues, are hired later in life than men, are given less prestigious churches, and are often overlooked in the hiring process of church leadership positions.[1]

Based on these stats, there are many churches operating in conflict with their prescribed egalitarian values by not elevating women to lead pastoral positions, or offering them equal treatment. When an individual promotes one value but acts in the opposite manner, this creates cognitive dissonance and instability for the individual. The same can be said for an organization. When an organization subscribes to a set of principles and values but leads in a way that does not reflect those principles, this creates confusion and instability for the organization and its participants.

Barb, a successful corporate working mother of a blended family shared how she was excited to attend her local church with her new-found faith. It had been a real support for her struggling marriage and young kids, and she found her faith nurtured. Her spiritual growth and that of her family was evidenced in the reignited love they held for one another.

On Mother's Day, she attended her worship service and was shocked when the pastor asked only the stay-at-home moms to stand and be recognized. They were applauded and given a gift, while the working mothers were completely ignored.

The pastor then went on to deliver a sermon on pornography and the responsibility women have in exacerbating this issue in men.

Despite the past positive experiences, it only took this one disastrous service to communicate how devalued and unappreciated she was in the church. Her corporate job treated her with more respect, value, and admiration, and the discrimination laws and human resources department reinforced a culture of equity and respect. Yet this megachurch overlooked this cultural inconsistency and lost a valuable, educated, successful contributor to the church body and leadership. And, without the support she needed, Barb's marriage ended in divorce.

Although women comprise over half of the church membership, more women who were once active church participants are becoming "dechurched" than in times past. Research states 61 percent of all dechurched people are women.[2]

The Barna Group points to five reasons woman are excusing themselves from church: lack of priority, busyness, lack of emotional support, and changes in family structure and beliefs. Only 17 percent of women say they feel very supported within church, 23 percent say somewhat supported by church, and nearly half, 43 percent, say they don't feel any emotional support from the church. There has been an increase of atheism among women and even more so among millennial women.[3]

The disturbing statistics concerning women, juxtaposed with the significant lack of women pastors, provokes the question: is the American church making a positive impact on justice for women or are they reinforcing negative patriarchal beliefs, intentionally or unintentionally, that perpetuate this issue?

Like Jesus and the New Testament church, Christian men and women are to be society's influencers in advocating for the less fortunate, living in love with one another, and leading together harmoniously.

When women are viewed as inferior, it gives grounds for them to be treated as inferior. The financial and emotional cost of treating the abuse of women is a significant cost for society and provides a tragic legacy for a nation.

Culturally Delayed Churches

Contemporary churches have made significant strides in embracing egalitarian views for the genders since 1960-1970, as egalitarianism has had a growing influence throughout religious denominations and movements. For example, women in church leadership increased from 5 percent in the 1990s to 10 percent in 2009.[4]

But even with these gains, the church is still a far cry from embodying the equity for the genders it claims to hold, providing mixed messages and double binds for women and couples.

Ruth Haley Barton says, "For women who want to know God more deeply and to participate in shaping the next generation of women for Christ, there is nothing more important (aside from the issue of salvation) than knowing how God views us and whether we are free to serve him in the way that he calls us. The way we answer this question affects all areas of life: self-esteem, emotions, our relationships with husband, children, and parents, worship and service to God, and our view of ourselves at work and in society."[5]

Instead of blocking or marginalizing women leaders, churches need to be about empowering women to operate according to their abilities, talents, and education so they can make a significant impact on the church and future generations. Anything less is inconsistent with the heart and values of Christianity.

To understand how this culture is being reinforced and giving mixed messages to women of "we want you, but only if you behave this way," we need to look to our Christian education systems.

When I was in college, I was often told, "Wow, you would make a great pastor's wife." Not once did any of my professors encourage me to pursue ministry despite my heart for missions and church ministry. Nursing and education were the ideal roles for Christian women and subtly reinforced.

Several decades later, my daughter is still having the heated debated discussion of whether or not women can preach or teach in her egalitarian Christian university. Although many of her professors recognize and support her calling to ministry, many of the students and colleagues continue to challenge her spiritual right to join the ranks of male pastors. When she was exploring seminaries where she could study theology, she described only three significant seminaries on the West Coast that would even accept her due to her gender.

In Christian education, women comprise a majority of the undergraduates, yet only 5–7 percent of the senior leaders are female in Christian education.[6] The prominent and reputable Evangelical Theological Society (ETS) has approximately 4,500 members with women comprising only 6 percent of the membership. Evangelicalism has not afforded equity for women leadership positions as compared to secular circles or mainline church denominations. Restrictions on women teaching, preaching, and leading in church and seminaries are often promoted and reinforced among many evangelical churches.[7] Because of this, it is not uncommon for women to feel unwelcome, insecure, invisible, or unequal in churches or organizations promoting restrictive beliefs for women.

If we are to produce different churches who are inclusive of women and passionate about empowering women to be leaders and participants, in and out of the home as God has designed them to be, we must provide different education experiences. These must include more women leaders in senior positions, different classes promoting the value of women in church bodies, and platforms for differences of opinion to be openly and lovingly debated.

Most of all, we need to provide young minds the modeling and mentoring for men and women to work effectively and successfully together, in marriage, work, and leadership. Author and activist W.E.B. DuBois said, "Children learn more from what you are than what you teach."[8] What are we teaching our children by how we lead in our schools, churches, institutions, and marriages? This speaks louder than any book or lecture.

Society and Church Clashes

Statistics show that today's American couples prefer an egalitarian relationship.

In fact, one study out of the University of Texas and the University of California involving 329 unmarried men and women between the ages of 18–32 revealed that 94 percent desired an egalitarian relationship.[9] "Power couples," where both partners are educated and have careers, is on the rise from two decades ago, and couples have more egalitarian views and less stereotypical gender roles in the home.

In 2016, for the first time in American history, we had a woman candidate for president. We are seeing progressive efforts within women's movements and justice implemented for sexual abuse more than ever before in history. In this Era of Women, it is culturally blind that churches still operate in a detached cultural system that views theology and church leadership through the voices of men and teach theology through a patriarchal lens. The male bias is out of step with current cultural values, offering a delayed and offensive culture to many women and men holding egalitarian values.

Yet many evangelical churches are still consistently operating under patriarchal practices. Similar to the current practice in dynamic marriages, the contemporary church is facing challenges in implementing principles of equity to mirror their egalitarian beliefs. This tension creates a cultural delay and poor support for the evolving contemporary marriage.

Like marriages, churches can learn to change in order to better support our modern marriages. The symbiotic relationship of church and marriage requires the evolution of church leadership.

Coincidentally, change in churches can be influenced by our modern marriages with spouses learning to partner better together. In turn, church leadership can grow and shift in pursuing gender parity and equity thus providing a healthy and culturally relevant ethos for marriages.

And as we find it, both marriages and the church will reap the benefits as well.

CHAPTER 8

Peer Churches

As an increasing number of couples are growing their way into Peer Marriages, they often find themselves seeking out church communities, and if they are lucky, they will find themselves at a Peer Church.

Peer Marriages need supportive environments, and Peer Churches can provide them. In Peer Churches, similar to Peer Marriages, gender-balanced leadership functions according to giftedness and ability rather than gender. Just as Peer Marriages make the health of the marriage the top priority of both partners, Peer Churches make the church community the top priority—a place where both men and women are active, contributing members in building a flourishing community.

Instead of espousing outdated and divisive gender teachings, these churches use the works of contemporary marriage experts, popular psychology concepts, personal stories, and contemporary writers to positively influence marriages, while integrating gender-inclusive and unity-minded theology.

Neither church doctrine nor unity teachings are compromised in the effort to bring together a unified community.

Leadership positions are not selected according to gender, but according to giftedness and ability.

During an interview, former Willow Creek Church Lead Teaching Pastor Steve Carter described how the church developed a gender-balanced staff by "selecting leaders according to spiritual gifts, discovering how they were wired, and how to unleash them" into their church. He also talked about the value of "seeing the Imago Dei (image of God) in every person."[1] His words describe exactly what Peer Churches strive to do: value leaders based on ability and giftedness instead of assigning value according to gender.

And, as we've seen, there is vast biblical support for this. In fact, as the church was getting established in the Old Testament after the Israelites' departure from Egypt, we see a powerful display of men and women working according to their giftedness regardless of gender. Exodus 35:10, 29 says, "All who are skilled among you are to come and make everything the Lord has commanded. . . All the Israelite men and women who were willing brought to the Lord freewill offerings for all the work the Lord through Moses had commanded them to do."

The key phrase is *all who were willing*. There was no discrimination of gender or gender stereotypes, as we see men and women designing, building, and creating as they worked together to create the place of worship. This reflects the spirt of Peer Churches as they have a greater ability to operate in unity, peace, and love since hierarchical principles and practices are removed. This frees members to focus on doing what each does best to contribute to the health of the whole.

Peer Churches Offer Many Benefits to Peer Marriages

When marriages are thriving, they contribute to producing a healthy church culture, as both partner harmoniously thus influencing an ethos of equity. Peer Marriages offer a hopeful prospect for improving church culture and validate the statement "healthy marriages are the best way to build a healthy society."[2] The Peer Marriage model echoes the values of the original marriage of Adam and Eve as well as the spirit of the Acts church: "All the believers were together and had everything in common" (Acts 2:44). There was no discrimination between the genders as equity, love, and generosity created unity among the believers.

When partners like Pete and Shelly, who are in a Peer Marriage, attend a Peer Church, they want to see their marriage value among the genders mirrored in the leadership at church. They understand the value of operating with equity in the relationship and the distresses they experienced when the power was imbalanced in the marriage. They don't want to go backwards and desire a spiritual environment that helps them progress in developing unity and partnership for their Peer Marriage.

Today, the majority of evangelical men help with parenting and household duties, and more married evangelical women are employed outside of the home. Therefore, Peer Churches are a more culturally relevant climate for contemporary marriages. In Peer Churches, traditional roles are discarded as participants operate according to their ability, expertise, training, and giftedness regardless of gender. This provides a supportive culture for modern marriages, and aligns with theological principles for the church to operate as a body in Christ with everyone playing their part: "From him the whole body, joined and held together by every supporting ligament, grows and builds itself up in love, as each part does its work" (Ephesians 4:16).

Couples in Peer Marriages who attend Peer Churches experience another blessed alliance as they both operate with shared values, developing an ethos of mutuality within their marriages and churches. This creates a congruent culture that empowers Peer Marriages to thrive within the context of the Peer Church. There is no cognitive dissonance as the beliefs and behavior of both marriages and churches are harmoniously aligned.

Near Peer Churches

Unfortunately sometimes in their search for a Peer Church, couples can unknowingly find themselves attending a Near Peer Church, where egalitarian beliefs are promoted yet hierarchical beliefs are practiced.

When this happens, the couple may experience a spiritual optical illusion of sorts, breeding confusion for the marriage. And for good reason! Adam and Eve themselves would have been disappointed with Near Peer Churches as they longed for the harmonious, equitable community experienced in Eden.

Near Peer Churches, similar to Near Peer Marriages, promote egalitarian views but do not operate from the principles of mutuality. They may claim to have egalitarian principles, but operate with patriarchal or hierarchical values. They may *say* that they value women in leadership (and even promote it in their bylaws) all while holding patriarchal values that restrict women from gaining power or from being seen or heard.

Near Peer Churches give mixed messages and continually place people in double binds as they teach theology specifically packaged for a bygone era and apply it for contemporary marriages.

One female lead pastor found herself in a Near Peer Church when she was hired at Nazarene Church in California. As one of the main speakers of a Missio Alliance Conference, she described the lose-lose situations she encountered in pastoring at her church. Although she was ordained by the Nazarene denomination, which supports women pastors as based on their theological doctrine, she experienced strong opposition as lead pastor due to her gender, and many long-time members left the church.

She was conflicted, angry, and confused at the inconsistencies as she noted the theology teachings and practices had shifted from their original and stated theological doctrine. The Nazarene doctrine and theology on the role of women includes "the right of women to use their God-given spiritual gifts within the church and affirms the historic right of women to be elected and appointed to places of leadership" and that "no human being is to be regarded as inferior on the basis of social status, race, or gender."[3]

Despite these clearly stated beliefs, women were not supported in operating in positions of leadership as evidenced by the significant struggles she experienced. Yet, through the support of her leaders, she was able to attract younger crowds who resonated with the gender-balanced staff and provide opportunities for women leaders, as she created a more culturally relevant environment for Peer Marriages. As a result, she was able to transform a Near Peer Church back to its Peer Church values.

Near Peer Churches are facing issues with embodying the egalitarian values in leadership training, marital therapy, marriage classes, and relationship enhancement classes. This cognitive dissonance in church culture, where they believe one thing and do another, is creating confusion and instability for the church body as well as Peer Marriages.

Similarly, it can be reasoned when Peer couples attend Near Peer Churches they experience cognitive dissonance as the church says one thing and does another, creating instability for both marriage and church.

Mixed Messages for Marriages

These mixed messages and double binds provoke confusion and frustration for the marriages seeking a spiritually supportive culture.

Near Peer Churches elicit conflict, tension, and confusion for both genders and both institutions of marriage and church. Unrealistic expectations are set for marriage as roles are based on gender rather than giftedness. These expectations confuse and dysregulate marriages and require each partner to operate according to gender roles instead of personality styles and ability.

Jim and Karen, for example, believed what their church taught that men are the spiritual leaders in the church and at home. They attended counseling for their troubled marriage, and the church counselor reinforced these beliefs. Unfortunately, James would have to make some profound and extreme personality changes if he were to fit the divine role of "head of the home." Sadly, Karen expressed disappointment that James fell short of the ideal complementarian model, and their marriage lived in a constant state of unresolved shame, disappointment, and despair.[4]

When unrealistic ideals are placed on marriages and the relational companionship is replaced with a hierarchical leadership, it diminishes the authenticity of the relationship. This cognitive dissonance for the marriage partners provokes instability, unresolved shame, and perpetual conflict for the marriages. In turn, it produces a theologically and psychologically unstable foundation for both institutions of marriage and church.

Stifled Femininity

A consequence of the fall for Eve was that her voice became stifled as her power diminished. If Adam and Eve could devise a church that replicated what they'd lost in the fall, I believe they would want one that validated both of their voices and reinstate both to their original, divine place of power.

When women's voices are invalidated through patriarchalism the effects can be far-reaching and impacting to both genders. With patriarchalism in play, the value of a woman and her voice decreases.

Misinterpreted scripture and bible passages taken out of context create a huge barrier to women's voices getting heard in church and open the door for mistreatment of women. Tragically, studies reveal that increased aggression on women is prevalent where women are considered inferior citizens in any system or culture.[5]

Invalidating the woman's voice through ignoring, critiquing, interrupting, countering, belittling, dismissing, and offering unsolicited "helpful" suggestions are all considered covert abuse, which further oppresses the woman's power by minimizing her voice.

When women leaders' voices are rejected, they often develop public or outer voices that get accepted, while their authentic selves and their inner voices remain stagnant or undeveloped, thus compromising their strength and clarity. Fragmented, they are limited from leading authentically with men in marriage or church.

Recovering a true identity in Christ and healing from faulty thinking cause women to lead from their true selves, or wholeness instead of their woundedness. Churches can be influential in advocating for gender parity in churches and providing a space for women's voices to be respected, so as to foster healthy women leaders in leadership and marriage.

Lack of Feminine Leadership Traits

When female leadership is muted, the leadership trait of mothering, which benefits any organization, is lacking. Mothering can be defined as "a relationship and an activity; it brings together being and doing. It is about having responsibility for another."[6] The elements of mothering are entirely unique to a woman and few can replicate the pure maternal instincts as effectively as a woman. The care a woman gives is special and unique, and is evidenced by how she talks, shares, listens, and nurtures.[7]

Social theorist Julia Kristeva remarks on the impact of mothering on society through her theories of maternal ethics. She credits maternal instincts with having significant influence on social development within a society.[8] When the woman's voice is dismissed from leadership, the maternal instincts and nurturance unique to women is also dismissed and the institutions of marriage and church experience a significant loss of care.

Similarly, the mothering traits attributed to God are diminished and ignored, offering an insufficient and inaccurate image of the character of God. A beautiful divine feminine image describes God as a mother hen gathering her chicks under her wings (Matthew 23:37). Throughout scripture, God is described as a nursing mother, mother bear, comforting mother, and a mother in labor when describing deep maternal love for people.[9] The tender relationship between the Psalmist and God is depicted as such: "But I have calmed and quieted myself, I am like a weaned child with its mother; like a weaned child I am content" (Psalm 131:2). Undeniably, the triune God values the maternal characteristics of divinity.

When organizations believe that women are ill-suited for leadership positions, they provide a gender bias in their culture and compromise the authentic image of God. The church culture is called to be one of unity and equity, offering respect to all regardless of their gender. Mirroring anything less is reflecting the worldly values Christians are called to separate from. This is a far cry from the original divine design in the garden days, suggesting it is time for an update in Near Peer churches desiring to be Peer Churches. Like Near Peer Marriages, this update can be accomplished through blending theology and psychology to develop better character in leaders creating healthier communities.

Peer /Near Peer Church Assessment

Is the church you attend or lead a true Peer Church or a Near Peer Church? The following assessment can help you determine the answer to this question.

Peer/Near Peer Church Assessment

1. ☐ Yes ☐ No   Do both genders hold or are eligible for the highest titles in the organization?

2. ☐ Yes ☐ No   Do women preach in the main services?

3. ☐ Yes ☐ No   Are there designated spaces where only men can speak or lead?

4. ☐ Yes ☐ No   Are women leaders paid equally to male counterparts?

5. ☐ Yes ☐ No   Is there a place for women to come to the table and give leadership influence in all areas that men are allowed in?

6. ☐ Yes ☐ No   Is there gender-balanced leadership with pastoral or leadership positions?

7. ☐ Yes ☐ No   Do you use gender-inclusive bibles?

8. ☐ Yes ☐ No   Are women bible characters or
                  inspirational female illustrations
                  included in messages?

9. ☐ Yes ☐ No   Is career advancement mentoring
                  available for women?

10. ☐ Yes ☐ No   Do male leaders identify qualified
                  women in their congregation to put into
                  leadership?

11. ☐ Yes ☐ No   Are the male leaders active in pursuing
                  qualified, female leaders?

12. ☐ Yes ☐ No   Are ordained female ministers who are
                  church members used in the church
                  body?

13. ☐ Yes ☐ No   Are Christian women leaders in the
                  community pursued and validated for
                  what they can offer?

14. ☐ Yes ☐ No   Is there equal advancement opportunity
                  for both genders?

15. ☐ Yes ☐ No   Do the bylaws claim values that church
                  practices reflect?

16. ☐ Yes ☐ No   Are women pursued as elders and/or
                  hold lead pastoral positions according to
                  the bylaws?

17. ☐ Yes ☐ No   Is gender-inclusive terminology used in the values and bylaws?

18. ☐ Yes ☐ No   Are women included in conversations? Do they receive eye contact, introductions, equal talk time, affirmation, respect for their opinions?

19. ☐ Yes ☐ No   When male leaders use sarcasm, stereotypes, and objectifying humor to marginalize and invalidate female leaders, are they corrected?

20. ☐ Yes ☐ No   Do male leaders express healthy boundaries and a need for female pastors alongside male pastors?

21. ☐ Yes ☐ No   Are male leaders who make inappropriate advances or have inappropriate relationships with women held accountable for their behavior and disciplined appropriately?

22. ☐ Yes ☐ No   Is there a formal procedure for women to report if they are feeling disrespected, marginalized, unheard, or mistreated in the church community?

23. ☐ Yes ☐ No   When women ask for help to be advanced, protected, and mentored, do they receive that help?

24. ☐ Yes ☐ No   Do both genders have equal access to the stage?

25. ☐ Yes ☐ No   Are women actively pursued for pastoral positions and trained for leadership positions?

26. ☐ Yes ☐ No   Does the marriage curriculum or education reflect egalitarian values or complementarian, patriarchal, hierarchical values?

27. ☐ Yes ☐ No   Is theology taught with gender inclusivity?

28. ☐ Yes ☐ No   Are both genders represented in the Trinity?

29. ☐ Yes ☐ No   If pictures or plaques are in the church honoring past members, do they represent both genders?

30. ☐ Yes ☐ No   Do male leaders show integrity by promising to help privately and act as promised publicly?

31. ☐ Yes ☐ No   Do leaders apologize for unfair treatment and make amends by creating equity, justice, and psychological safety for women?

32. ☐ Yes ☐ No   Are there opportunities for men leaders to mentor women leaders appropriately?

33. ☐ Yes ☐ No — Do women in leadership feel free to express their opinions and advocate for equitable treatment?

34. ☐ Yes ☐ No — Are women leaders empowered to advocate for other women leaders and girls?

35. ☐ Yes ☐ No — Are women and men held accountable for immoral or disrespectful behavior that would hurt the body?

36. ☐ Yes ☐ No — Are there trainings on sexual harassment, emotional manipulation, and covert abuse or anything that prevents gender parity from thriving in the church?

37. ☐ Yes ☐ No — Is there an expressed value for equity between the genders in church messages and culture?

38. ☐ Yes ☐ No — Are there staff discussions on how to be more inclusive and develop gender parity in every service?

39. ☐ Yes ☐ No — Are women credited publicly and privately for their ideas, solutions, and contributions?

40. ☐ Yes ☐ No — Is equal talk space given to women and men in meetings?

41. ☐ Yes ☐ No — When hiring staff is gender balance a consideration?

42. ☐ Yes ☐ No   When there is a conflict with a woman, do you approach the woman instead of going through her husband?

43. ☐ Yes ☐ No   Are women acknowledged in greeting time or social interactions, the same as men?

44. ☐ Yes ☐ No   Are women thanked and appreciated for their perspectives and value expressed for their differences?

45. ☐ Yes ☐ No   When women speak, are they heard, helped, and honored for what they feel and need?

46. ☐ Yes ☐ No   Do women leaders get supported, or excused from leadership activities for having or caring for children?

47. ☐ Yes ☐ No   Do male leaders get supported, or excused from leadership activities for wanting to decrease professional time to care for children?

48. ☐ Yes ☐ No   Is there flexibility in your positions that allow women to parent, nurse, and work, and for men to parent and support their wives' careers?

49. ☐ Yes ☐ No   Are roles assigned by giftedness instead of gender?

50. ☐ Yes ☐ No   Are there any women pastors on staff to fill out this assessment?

Scoring:

If you answered 40-50 questions with "no" then this is a Non-Peer Church.

If you answered 15-39 of the questions with "no" then this is considered a Near Peer Church.

If you answered 14 or fewer of the questions with "no" then this is a Peer Church.

SECTION 2

CREATE | THE PATHWAY HOME

CHAPTER 9

Create Healthy Community

PART 1:
CREATE COMMUNITY IN MARRIAGE AND THE HOME

Be completely humble and gentle; be patient,
bearing with one another in love. Make every effort
to keep the unity of the Spirit through the bond of
peace. There is one body and one Spirit, just as you
were called to one hope when you were called; one
Lord, one faith, one baptism; one God and Father
of all, who is over all and through all and in all.
(Ephesians 4:2–5)

After the fall, Adam and Eve had to learn *how to* develop the desired, divine community they'd once had for themselves. They also needed to learn how to develop good character so they could partner, parent, and live in healthy community once again.

Knowing how to develop healthy community is easier for us than it was for Adam and Eve. Today, we've had centuries of philosophers, social scientists, and thought leaders to draw from in how to develop better communities. We have entire careers and extensive knowledge devoted to educating people on how to develop sustaining communities. We have books, websites, and curriculums to teach about good character. Organizations are encouraged to develop core values, and mission and vision statements. Leadership coaches are hired to promote healthy leadership in churches and organizations. Adam and Eve had zilch, zero, nada. They had to figure this out on their own, all the while grieving the loss of their perfect relationship and existence. What a culture shock this must have been for them!

As a therapist and social scientist, I have devoted my life to helping people develop healthy relationships and communities. Let me introduce some of my favorite relationship experts who have influenced me in my work and personal life to develop better communities.

Good Community Requires Intentional Living

God lives in community or family with Jesus and the Holy Spirit. He is a triune God who operates in oneness and harmonious community as each partner serves the others respectfully. Adam and Eve had to relearn how to do community that was harmonious and equitable in their marriage before they could experience it or teach it in church. When they could reclaim a harmonious, equitable partnership between themselves, they could live it out in larger communities.

Men and women are still learning how to cross the great divide to reconnect harmoniously with one another. Whether in the home, work, or church, conflict and competition between the genders is never taught but rather inherited. We need creativity and expert teaching to close the gender gap in leadership and create an equitable, compatible partnership between men and women. This single endeavor will provide huge job security for me as a therapist and leadership coach.

One way to achieve this in marriages is to utilize the work of relationship experts and behavioral scientists. By using developed models, theories, and philosophies as agents of change in creating more gender harmony, behavioral therapists are able to facilitate positive changes in bringing men and women together. What works in the home to create equity between men and women will also work in leadership positions for churches and organizations desiring gender parity. First, we'll explore how Near Peer Marriages can transition to Peer Marriages. Secondly, we'll apply these concepts to develop Near Peer Churches into Peer Churches.

Near Peer Marriages Evolving to Peer Marriages
To relieve the conflict, couples in these Near Peer Marriages often seek out therapy to foster a culture of equity. One popular therapeutic model developed by relationship expert John Gottman teaches couples how to foster a culture of mutuality through the Sound House Relationship Model. In his model, he outlines seven stages in which a couple or organization goes through before they can get a shared culture together. The pillars supporting the house are trust and commitment, which

are the support beams for the house. The first four stages are all about building a strong connection: developing love maps, sharing fondness and admiration, turning toward each other, and sharing a positive perspective, before they can even enter the fifth stage of managing conflict successfully. In the sixth stage, it's all about helping make life dreams come true, which culminates in the seventh stage of having a shared meaning or culture together.[1] Through research, this model has proven to be so effective, the Relational Sound House Model was adapted for organizations.[2]

Many times we are trying to resolve conflict when there is a poor foundation, knowledge, or respect for the other person or team. We need to feel safe, loved, accepted, and appreciated by the other person to be successful at conflict resolution and create a shared culture of equity. Too many times we are racing to develop a team without taking the time to develop a loving, meaningful connection. Then the conflict happens and we are not able to regulate or navigate it successfully because of the lack of positive foundation.

Bill and Jackie came to therapy because their children left home. Their marriage had always been defined by the kids' activities, and now that they were gone, Bill and Jackie weren't sure who they were as a couple anymore. As they sat on my couch with a pillow between them, no part of them touching, and complete avoidance of eye contact, I could cut the tension with a knife.

They used to have rip-roaring fights, but they learned to live amicably with each other by avoiding each other through staying busy with work, community, church, and family activities. Now with the kids gone, they were fighting often and arguing about every little thing. Where they used to laugh together over a little ribbing, they now remained stony and stoic. They snapped at one another for making mistakes and were quick to blame one another when things went awry. They felt lonely, angry, guarded, and uncertain about their relationship, but they had already put in over twenty years together, so they decided to try some therapy to see if I could help them with the perpetual fighting.

When I asked about the last time they went on a date or vacation together just the two of them, they stared blankly at me. When I asked what they enjoyed doing together, again I could hear crickets. Finally, I asked each what their partner's favorite color or food was, and again, the silence was deafening. They knew nothing about each other, and the years of avoiding each other did not prepare them to fight productively together. They assumed the worst, and any little comment became the ammunition for building their increasing negative narrative about each other. I gave them their homework: take a vacation from fighting and start working on playing and affirming one another. I used my mom's rule: "If you can't say anything nice, don't say anything at all." They were to go on two dates before their next appointment, and say at least three affirming comments to each other a day—nothing negative, or they charged each other $1.

In the next session, there was a noticeable difference. They sat closer to each other with no pillow between them, gave each other more eye contact, expressed humor with gentle teasing, and just seemed to be more at ease. After checking in they shared how they both had been affirming to each other daily, with only one $1 charge to Jackie for making a negative, critical comment to Bill. With the friendship slowly returning, we were able to learn some healthy resolution skills and tackle a small issue, and end the session with three affirmations to one another. As time progressed, Bill and Jackie came to know and enjoy each other again and assumed the best so their fights became manageable. They realized the importance of maintaining a respectful friendship so they could resolve fights easier and get back to enjoying one another.

Reality Therapy

Reality Therapy is built on the ideology of control theory and helps couples explore, identify, and meet the five primary needs of love/belonging, power/control, freedom, fun, and safety.[3] Friendship is considered paramount as each pursues their own needs as well as those of their partner, developing a relationship of mutuality.[4] According to this therapy, when the needs go unmet, partners suffer emotionally, psychologically, and relationally. Theorist William Glasser stresses the importance of getting these needs in order to have a happy and fulfilling life, and help meet the needs in your partner and others.

I see the five primary needs of Reality Therapy a bit differently. I see how love provides power, freedom, fun, and safety. When we have love, we have the security and ability to release others from the constraints of the expectations we hold over them. We allow freedom and fun to flourish as we enjoy being with people instead of working at controlling who we want them to be.

Seth and Mackenzie were married for fifteen years and had four children together. They lived a traditional marriage where she cared for the kids, and he provided for the family. Both were involved in raising the family and each had there designated roles. Mackenzie came to see me because she had recently gone back to work part-time and could not stop crying. With tears in her eyes she said, "I lost me, and I don't know how to find me." I asked her what she does for play, and she said, "Sleep."

To discover what she did for play, we had to take a walk down memory lane. Although she had loved playing the violin, she had stopped playing in high school. She loved choir, music, and going to concerts but had also stopped doing any of that in her dating days. Currently, she was teaching music part time, and she realized she was grieving the years she lost out on having fun and playing her music. In the hustle and bustle of marriage and kids, she forgot to play and considered it a luxury. To retrieve her emotional stability, she took up playing music again and making time to meet one of her very important missing needs of fun and play.

In Near Peer Marriages, it is common for one person to have more of their needs met at the expense of their partner's. A husband may be very good at meeting his play needs of fishing, golf, or working out, while the wife continues to pick up the extra load as he plays and she neglects her own play needs. All humans, male and female alike, need to be able to have these needs met, or emotional and relational instability threatens the climate in their marriages. There is no difference in families, churches, or communities. Meeting the needs of every individual improves the health of the whole community.

PART 2:
CREATE COMMUNITY IN CHURCHES

"In order to facilitate this inner vision we must first clear the way for the faculty of seeing. How this is to be done without psychology, that is, without making contact with the psyche, is, frankly, beyond my comprehension."

—Carl Jung[5]

Evolving a Near Peer Marriage to a Peer Marriage demands time, skill, commitment, and desire. Marriage therapists are constantly confronted with the challenge of helping contemporary couples develop the desired egalitarian concepts they are sorely lacking but desperately desiring. With the constant dynamic evolution of contemporary marriages, marital therapies struggle to fit the changing needs of couples. Therefore, marriage therapists have had to be innovative with therapeutic concepts and techniques to meet the unique needs of modern couples. Popular therapy techniques primarily used for individual therapy, such as solution-focused, attachment theory, and Emotion-Focused Therapy (EFT), are also being adapted for couples.[6] If marriage therapists need to shift in their therapeutic modalities and techniques to better assist contemporary couples, churches may also want to consider implementing new strategies in order to create a positive shift to better support Peer Couples.

Similarly, Near Peer Churches desiring to be Peer Churches can utilize psychological therapeutic techniques and egalitarian principles to establish equity in church leadership. Culture change expert James Hunter writes, "If we want to transform culture, what we actually have to do is get into the midst of the human cultural project and create some new cultural goods that reshape the way people imagine and experience their world. . . "[7] The new "cultural goods" are applying psychological marital therapeutic techniques integrated with faith principles to Near Peer Churches so as to transform culture.

The integration of theology with psychology or "Theopsych" can assist Near Peer Churches in developing a culture of desired structural integrity as they evolve to Peer Churches. Integrating theology with psychology to transform relationships and culture is often emphasized in the class content of Christian psychology programs. In addition to educating students and impacting their local community, Rosemead School of Biola University values serving the church by "educating the Christian community about the interface between faith and psychology" and considers this to be responsible stewardship of their psychological resources.[8]

Inserting psychology models and theories in a faith community offers a contemporary solution and promising method to transform Near Peer Church cultures. We will explore psychologist John Gottman's Sound Relationship House Model, used on marriages and later adapted for organizations, as a tool for developing Peer Churches.

The Sound Relationship Workplace Model

Just as Bill and Jackie had to learn how to build a Sound Relationship House and develop a healthy friendship in order to create a shared culture, so too a church needs to learn how to develop healthy relationships in order to have unity. The Sound House Model has been adapted for organizations with the Sound Relationship Workplace Model.

John Gottman's Sound Relationship House Model is an exemplary, scientifically researched therapeutic tool designed to assist couples and organizations in developing a shared culture of equity and fulfillment.[9]

Churches can implement this Sound Relationship Workplace model in order to develop a shared culture of mutuality.[10] Teaching the seven stages of the model to church leadership can empower them to build a healthy, shared culture, and foster this ethos within the church body. Seeking the services of an organizational coach or consultant who implements this model and other research based methods would be a worthy investment for a church desiring an inclusive, unified culture.

Developing a Peer Church Using the Sound Relationship Workplace Model

Churches have a hard time evolving into Peer Churches if the married couples leading the churches or organizations are in Near Peer Marriages.

Remember Max and Sandra, introduced in Chapter 5? They had to turn their marriage from a Near Peer to a Peer Marriage by operating according to their passions and abilities versus their gender stereotypes. It's challenging to create gender parity in the church or workplace if you haven't created it in the home. As married co-pastors, Max and Sandra[11] shared the responsibilities for pastoring the church and parenting their two children. Max described how he personally demoted himself from full-time pastor so his wife could be promoted to co-pastor. This significant leadership model may not have transpired if one of the team members had not had an open dialogue with Max and Sandra, which set the stage for continued dialogues to openly discuss the gender struggles in the home and church.

With the leadership values for gender parity in place at home and in the church, the leadership team was able to focus on leadership and culture development reflecting the church's core values, and vision and mission statements. To foster a shared culture, the Sound Relationship Workplace model was used for leadership training.[12] This influenced every leadership area of the church: in leadership development, teaching, greeting, marketing, and culture development. Principles of equity and inclusivity of church members were applied to church leadership and culture development. Practically, the church became intentional about representing equity among the genders and minorities in worship services.

They discovered when they applied the Sound Relationship Workplace model to church leadership and culture development, gender parity was developed. A surprising secondary gain was the inclusivity and unity achieved across denominations, classes, races, and minority groups. When men and women come together, a culture of equity and inclusivity can be established for all. Discrimination does not stay localized to one gender, class, or group. It is contagious and spreads like a deadly disease infecting the body and preventing a sense of oneness whether in the home or church. Similarly, loving connection is also contagious as it spreads its culture of equity, empathy, and oneness influencing the hardest of hearts to live with harmony and peace.

Reality Therapy and Churches

From the perspective of Reality Therapy, churches can understand the five primary needs of every human. They can work as a cohesive body by encouraging people to cultivate loving, positive friendships, establish more power and control in their lives by providing empowering and equitable teaching for both genders, and fostering a playful, joyful culture. This echoes the primary purposes of the church to exhort one another, build each other up in love, and to be joyful.[13] We all want love, power, control, and freedom to express these needs with security.

In 2 Timothy 1:7, God tells us he did not give us the spirit of fear, but of power, love, and discipline. We are called and given the spirit to fight fear and cultivate power, love, and a peaceful, secure environment where we can bond securely together. We are given the power to live in love in both our marriages and our churches. We just need to choose to take the power to love.

Fear is the greatest enemy of securing a culture of equity. It produces a mentality of scarcity causing greed to be the fuel for getting our basic emotional needs met. As we fight for what we need to survive, the hormone adrenaline kicks in, activating the sympathetic system or the fight/flight/freeze responses to guide our reactions. Love cultivates a spirit of generosity where honor is the fuel to ensure there is enough to share so all needs can be met. Love activates the hormone oxytocin, which is the bonding hormone that tends, befriends, and bonds us to those around us. Seeing the uniformity of needs in every human, regardless of gender, builds a culture of compassion and understanding fueled by love and grace. The alternative is to build an environment cultivated by fear thus developing a culture of judgement and condemnation, fueled by fear and shame.

As a pastor's kid, I enjoyed the love and grace of a church that acted as extended family. So many dear faces and friends come to mind who met my needs for loving and belonging as they functioned as aunties, grandmas, sisters, and moms. There were great men who lovingly teased, encouraged, and mentored me to be the leader and person I am today. Softball games, pool parties, after-church ice cream runs, youth group activities, camps, and late-night teepeeing adventures are the happy memories of church life.

But with that closeness came conflict. From a young age I was aware of the perpetual controversies among members of organ versus piano, pews versus chairs, and hymns versus choruses. The reactions to fear were shocking to me as I saw grown adults act in ways even my nine-year-old self knew were very inappropriate. One time, a member angry about choruses being sung instead of hymns, hid and locked up the coffee pots for donut hour just to make a point sending the refreshment team into a tizzy. Everyone knows you never mess with donut hour and the coffee!

My childhood church had wonderful people and vision. But the conflict felt looming and ever present. My dad was

finally fired after three attempts. As fate would have it, the
dissenters won by two votes, and just like that, my dad's twelve-
year ministry at Community Church of Palm Springs came to a
close. Within two weeks, we left the place I called home, where
I learned about God and called people "family." I find it ironic
that this sanctuary was leveled and condos stand in its place. The
fellowship hall remains as a historical monument to this day. To
me, it serves as a historical warning of what happens when fear
is allowed to fuel an organization rather than love. Fear brings
death while love brings life. Some churches and relationships
are so consumed and infiltrated by fear, I do believe they need
to die so something else can be birthed. I think God makes it
quite clear how we are to be known: by our love.

Heterarchy Leadership Model in the Church

A culture or system must undergo "depatriarchalization"[14]
if a new leadership model is to thrive. Otherwise, competing
values vie for leadership.

In Max and Sandra's church, leadership became designated
according to giftedness rather than gender. The leadership team
was organized according to their strengths as identified through
the Strengths Finder Test.[15] After assessing the team's strengths,
I introduced a Heterarchy leadership model (instead of a
Hierarchical model) and coached them on implementing this
leadership model. We used the Sound Relationship Workplace
model as a concrete model to make this shift. "Heterarchy may
be defined as the relation of elements to one another when they
are unranked or when they possess the potential for being ranked
in a number of different ways."[16] It is also "both a structure and

a condition."[17] The head leaders operate as facilitators as they guide and organize the leadership vision and abilities of the leadership team and parishioners, and interchange as leaders. Equity, unified vision, compassionate connections, and trust are all key elements to embracing the Heterarchy model and creating a shift from hierarchical to heterarchical leadership style.

Dr. Pepper Schwartz heralded the Heterarchy form of leadership in an interview. "Consensus is a more powerful tool," she said, and "all responses and ideas have the right to surface."[18] By implementing the Heterarchy model, and utilizing therapeutic principles and modalities, Max and Sandra are creating a church where everyone can have a place at the table, regardless of their ethnicity, class, or gender. I recommend soliciting the services of a skilled coach, consultant, or counselor to provide the outside perspective and expertise to make this leadership shift in your church as peacefully and skillfully as possible.

A Country's Response to Patriarchy

In parts of north-central Kenya patriarchalism is a way of life and women live under a harsh system. Traditional views of Samburuian men about women are, they need to be controlled, can't lead themselves, are property to be owned, traded, bought, or killed. Women have no rights. Although female circumcision was banned in 2011, it is believed 80 percent of the Samburuian brides still undergo the procedure and are deemed unmarriable without it.[19] In response, several matriarchal villages are cropping up. In 1990 a sisterhood of fifteen fed-up women raped by British soldiers took matters into their own hands.

They bought some land from the government and started their village complete with its economy, culture, and education system in the Samburu District.[20] Umoja means "unity" in Swahili and it is a village led and developed by women for a refuge and haven for mistreated and sexually abused females in their region. No men are allowed to live there. The women build their own houses, provide schools for their children, and make money based on the beads they sell.[21]

Rebecca, the chairlady and friend of Hilary Clinton, describes how men want to destroy the village due to the threat Umoja brings to the Samburu culture and traditions. When the wives would make money, the men would beat up the women and take the money. In protest, she continues her village that has grown to about fifty women and two hundred children.[22] With an easy frankness, she says, "Let them kill us and make a story of killing all of the women in this village." Her boldness and bravery to empower and reclaim the dignity of women is admirable. "When they call us women it is like a dirty name. We walk, and we talk, and we laugh. Let us show them we are happy and we have to be proud we are women."[23]

Just a bit north, another matriarchal village Nachami is run by women but men are allowed to live there. Mary the chairlady says: "We still have our husbands because we never separated at heart." Although poverty led them to start the village, women hold the power in the village because "it is the women who brought men here, and they hold firmly to the belief "there is nothing they can do without us." In order for men to live in Nachami they must reject the Samburu principles and agree to a new way of living and thinking. Male resident,

Ebo says, "I don't want to be more greater than her. I want us to do the same. When we work, we work the same."

Although Ebo lives in a third-world country, he can easily be described as a modern man pioneering a new path for the next generation and current western cultures. The message of equality is spreading to younger generations as younger men are joining the cause to live equitably with women. One enlightened male resident claimed how he grew to reject the damaging traditional practices of our culture through education.

Female genital mutilation and inequitable treatment of women will not be eradicated but nor will any inequitable treatment be eliminated in any culture without education. Without education, tradition makes the rules for human behavior regardless of how harmful it is to the group members. Nachami means "love." Ebo sums this up simply "So we love each other." Learning how to love one another is an education requiring the voices and leadership of both genders.

In 2015, President Obama's visit to Kenya put women's rights to the forefront of a national dialogue. "Around the world there is a tradition of repressing women, treating women and girls as second class citizens. Those are bad traditions. They need to change. There's no reason young girls should suffer genital mutilation. There's no place in civilized society for the early or forced marriage of children. These traditions may date back centuries, they have no place in the twenty-first century." Just because practices have been treasured traditions doesn't always mean they are worth passing on. Church communities desiring unity fueled by love need to consider letting go of antiquated, culturally irrelevant traditions preventing oneness and equity in a church body.

CHAPTER 10

Create Healthy Character

Good Character Develops Good Community

Developing healthy character is a great strategy for ensuring a healthy community of diversity with unity, otherwise known as Peer Culture. By creating a Peer Culture, both marriages and churches can move from a Near Peer status to a Peer status with Peer Marriages and Peer Churches complementing each other harmoniously. This is like the good ol' garden days.

Our calling as Christians, simply put, is to develop healthy character so we can become one united force to change our world. We are better together. Whether in marriage or church, we are called to cultivate oneness that does not eliminate the individual diversity and uniqueness of each person, but rather utilizes the diversity to complement our unity. Differences rarely create unity unless we are intentional about appreciating the differences and have common goals and vision in mind to collectively and collaboratively focus our differences toward. God's Spirit is here to guide us, and our will and self-determination must be engaged as we seek to live according to the values and character we are designed to live by.

Theologian and author Jo Saxton says character is more important than gifts, skills, calling, or ability. She defines character as:

> ". . . who you are on the inside, your personality, your emotional maturity, your personal integrity, your attitudes, your values and worldview. Your character carries your strength and your weaknesses, your wholeness and your brokenness. Your character is shaped by events and experiences, fashioned by your personal relationships, influenced by the culture around you. If you're serious about leadership and godly influence, then we need to pay close attention to your character."[1]

Too many times Christian or religious leaders are preoccupied with establishing the religious culture and advancing their church without heeding the importance of developing character in themselves, their marriages, and their church community.

Personal Quest for Community

I also know many Christians can identify with deep wounds from marriage and the church community because of poor character choices of individuals. With nearly half of Americans unchurched, church researchers are discovering people who are leaving traditional churches to pursue spiritual practices offering more alternative methods.[2] A growing trend is for people who "love Jesus but not the church" to develop their spirituality without practicing religion, and are considered dechurched as they have not attended church within six months or more. They hold a sincere faith but hold no allegiance to a local church, and the majority of these members at 61 percent are women.[3]

These counter-cultural movements could very well be in response to the discriminatory environments, unintentionally and intentionally, promoted by many evangelical churches. As the dechurched population grows and the church body shrinks, we desperately need some strategic plans to achieve a loving, peaceful, and unified community.

I've always been passionate about community and bringing people together collaboratively, to create a new thing with passion and purpose, especially if it means overturning the old to get something better and new. I love the thrill of innovating something beautiful from nothing. I guess I'm a revolutionary at heart.

As an identical twin, I've heard it said, "You get used to doing life with a second." So I suppose it's no surprise I did what most people do when they want to live in peaceful, loving, collaborative community. I got married, expecting to experience that peaceful partnership full of good will I always longed for. Yes, marital bliss existed primarily in my head. I often found myself at a loss as to how to communicate effectively and to "speak the truth in love" as our therapist continually promoted. Apparently, I feel my emotions passionately, and I have a vivid picture of my reality and a strong commitment to my perspective—all the makings of conflictive community if I can't be open-minded to the perspective of others.

To complicate matters, I am an educator turned social worker and marriage therapist, and I should know how to live and teach blissful community. When I became active in my local church, I also expected to have that blissful community experience. Over and over I found myself having glimpses of this coveted community but found it fleeting and lacking in collaborative consistency, as self-absorbed leaders promoted their own purposes, and moral failings became a common occurrence for water cooler talk. In my continued quest for healthy community I realized the character or the spirit of the individual is crucial to developing healthy community. So I went to seminary and received my Doctor of Ministry degree in Global Leadership to discover how to be a spiritually healthy leader so as to develop healthy communities.

I continued looking around for inspirational help with creating healthy community. Oprah was a beautiful inspiration. I wanted to live in community with Oprah! But since she didn't respond to my heartfelt email request, I had to look elsewhere.

Research and experiences are revealing that as a society, we are also struggling to connect in healthy and secure ways. With the increase of divorce, blended families, and media screen time, people are becoming increasingly detached, creating what psychologists identify as insecure, anxious, and disorganized attachment disorders.

We are forgetting how to connect or love as we are recovering from traumatic family break-ups and becoming lost in our smartphones. Texting and social media are becoming the standard mode of communication, as without voice tone, eye contact, and body language, we lose 93 percent of communication. As one adolescent client humorously related to me, "I forgot how to make a phone call on my phone, because all I do is text!"

Psychologists are reporting that approximately half of US society consider themselves poorly attached or disorganized attached,[4] meaning we don't connect well with each other. These people make up families, churches, and communities, and my concern is if we don't start to teach how to love by developing good character, we are vulnerable to replaying destructive, disorganized attachment in all relationships, thus perpetuating community dysfunction.

I continued to discover there were lots of issues with community and struggles for us all coming together everywhere. Denominational splits, rise of divorce in families, female abuse, school shootings, lack of affordable medical services, the mental health care crisis, and ethnicity division have all been on the rise and in the headlines of many newspapers. I was not alone—we are all having an issue developing stable community and "speaking the truth in love." Poor character development and broken attachments are making healthy communities a very challenging endeavor, at home, work, or church. From the micro to macro systems, it appears we are experiencing a community crisis on all levels.

Community Experts

Not to be deterred, I started looking to nature.

Who's doing community well? Bees. Look at the colonies

and communities that are doing community well. They are self-sacrificing, humble, collaborative, unity-minded, purposeful, and protective of the community working hard and achieving a sweet success. . . I found myself envious of the bees! I wanted to live in their perfect little hexagon homes, buzzing around, making sweet honey together. I realized their character was exceptional! Each seemed to be content doing their small part to make a healthy, thriving community.

How do we come together like the bees to create a healthy community with a sweet outcome? If the wee bees can do it, how much more can competent, intelligent humans develop good character and create good community with oneness? So I started asking, "Who is governing morality, teaching good character, and instruction on healthy spiritual virtues?" Spiritual communities. Churches, mosques, temples. Yet there is so much division with religion that all we have to do is look at history and current affairs to see the wars and conflicts religion creates.

I started to dream of a community revolution where we could develop healthy character to live out sweet community in our homes and beyond. I knew this would not be possible unless I could find some common ground to build my idealistic concept of developing stellar communities formed from healthy character.

The Common Characteristics
There has to be something we all agree on in our spiritual communities, various cultures, and as individuals to create healthy character so as to foster harmonious communities. I did

some research and made some powerful discoveries that could positively influence our marriages and spiritual communities to develop healthy character and live with equity and harmony. I was excited to discover we have some significant similarities that we can build on.

Six Spiritual Values

From my own Christian training, I knew Ephesians 4 listed out six key spiritual values for us to live by in order to develop healthy character and a unified community. These values allow us to be many individual parts designed for unique purposes but operate as one body. I was curious if these spiritual values were promoted beliefs in other religious groups. I researched the six major world religious groups:

- **Christianity**: 2.3 billion
- **Islam**: 1.8 billion
- **Hinduism**: 1.1 billion
- **Buddhism**: 500 million
- **Sikhism:** 27 million
- **Judaism:** 14 million[5]

I discovered the major religious groups all teach the same six spiritual values for their members to live by in order to develop healthy character to sustain a thriving community. They are the core tenets for character development of every major religious group and reinforced in their teachings, leadership, and community life. They are humility, gentleness, patience, love, unity, and peace.

Since these spiritual values are core beliefs in developing good character and healthy community in not only Christianity but other major religious groups, I have to believe they are essential traits to value and develop. If we can all live by this in our marriages, homes, places of worship, etc., we can unlock the secret to living with oneness. I believe it requires human desire along with some innovative methods, strategic planning, and the work of God's Spirit. If we are instructed to live in oneness, whether in marriage or in the church, and to live in a peaceful, loving community with one another, then it must be possible, and we must access any tool that can take us toward our ideal.

Six Character Virtues

In addition to the spiritual values we share, positive psychologists have identified six primary virtues that are present in all cultures. They are: wisdom, courage, humanity, transcendence, justice, and temperance or moderation.[6]

Positive psychologists Dr. Neal Mayerson, Dr. Martin Seligman, and Dr. Christopher Peterson understand the importance of developing character strengths and how it leads to a happier, purposeful, and fulfilled life.

In 2001, they established the VIA Character Institute because they understood that character was the key to understanding what is best about humans.[7] Through their research of cultures world-wide, they identified six primary virtues every culture values by asking people who they admire and why. There were twenty-four character strengths identified and filed under each virtue, while claiming all humans have all of these twenty-four strengths to varying degrees. In 2004, Seligman and Peterson co-authored a ground-breaking book on their research entitled *Character Strengths and Virtues.*[8] From this, they developed the VIA character strength test that identifies the strengths in each person.

The VIA personality profile test defines character strengths as "our positive personality in that they are our core capacities for thinking, feeling, and behaving in ways that can bring benefit to us and others."[9] As character is further developed, the ability to overcome problems, build better relationships, and enhance your overall well-being is the promising result. Unlike other personality tests that promote and focus on developing your ability deficits or personality weaknesses, the VIA Character Strengths Survey promotes capitalizing on your strengths and admiring these strengths in others to live their best life.

In order to build the six virtues, they encourage people to have a growth mindset versus a fixed mindset, such as exhibiting resiliency in response to rejection or failure. By choosing a growth mindset, we utilize the twenty-four character strengths to cultivate the six virtues. In other words, focusing on your strengths makes you stronger as focusing on the strengths of others makes them stronger, thus enhancing relationships and humanity as we all make a better version of ourselves together. Positive psychologists found the key to successful human relationships is appreciating the strengths in others, thus building a common language for us to develop more unity.[10]

Four Primary Relationships

Finally, social scientists have identified four primary relationships we all have and need to connect with and nurture in order to create healthy community: ourselves, God or a

Divine Being, others, and our earth. The psychological model teaching this is called the paradigm of unity."[11] This model theorizes we need to be connected and unified with the Divine, ourselves, others, and our earth in order to achieve unity. We cannot expect to establish unity with others when we are internally conflicted, confused about who or what we worship, or at odds with our environment. Just as we need to be aligned in our mind, body, and spirit for good mental health, so too we need to be connected collaboratively in our relationships with God, others, and our earth to have unity and one body. To reassure, perfection is never the goal with establishing healthy relational connection, but rather progress as fueled by insight, truth, and divine assistance.

So, here's my dream to address the relationship crises we find ourselves experiencing within the home and beyond: Create a community revolution by living with intention to develop strong character. Here's how: what if we commit as individuals and communities to live by the 6 spiritual values and develop the 6 character traits, while promoting a connectedness with our 4 primary relationships? How would this impact our marriages, homes, churches, communities, world? What could we accomplish if we learned to come together and live by building on our similarities and strengths? Within the religions communities alone, that would be 7.8 billion people living by their claimed spiritual values around the world. Our world would be a better place and maybe the bees would be envious of us.

To create a visual for these shared characteristics, I designed a model for how we can make this dream of a community revolution a reality.

Understanding the CommUNiTY Model

Healthy community is created by developing healthy character. I imagine Adam and Eve would have benefited from the CommUNiTY Model as it would have been reminiscent of their garden days. Both institutions of marriage and church can learn how to have unity and oneness, to be one body and to operate with unity with diversity.

The six key spiritual values are the lines of a hexagon, and each spiritual value is paired with one of the six virtues as the spiritual value is what fosters the corresponding human virtue. The four primary relationships needing alignment for unity fill the hexagon, as the ultimate goal of achieving one body holds the center.

This is what I refer to as hexagon strength, as this shape is considered one of the strongest and most efficient shapes to build and provide storage as evidenced by the bee's honeycomb. I spelled community like CommUNiTY as a reminder that the individual or the "i" is always present in community but not overemphasized in the spirit of developing healthy, inclusive, collaborative community.

The CommUNiTY Model

Living the CommUNiTY Model

Theological and psychological principles intertwined offer a powerful formula for maturing the human character. Yet human behavior, family origin, and society get in the way of instructing us who we should be as a human and how to treat the opposite gender. Without intentional living and divine intervention, we will continue to re-enact fallen living.

Let's learn how to live this model, and how each part intersects with the other. Starting with the spiritual values and the character virtues, I will explain how each impacts our relationships with God, self, others, and our earth.

HUMILITY

Virtue of Wisdom and Knowledge: Humility Invites Wisdom and Knowledge

When pride comes, then comes disgrace, but with humility comes wisdom. (Proverbs 11:2)

Walking with a Humble God

Who, being in very nature God, did not consider equality with God something to be used to his own advantage; rather, he made himself nothing by taking the very nature of a servant, being made in human likeness. And being found in appearance as a man, he humbled himself by becoming obedient to death—even death on a cross! (Philippians 2:5-8)

The level of humility Jesus displayed was unlike anything the world has ever seen. There is no greater example. The perfect Creator of humanity, the king of the universe, was born into a human body, raised by messy, imperfect humans, lived lovingly among them, and then allowed himself to be killed by them in one of the most humiliating deaths invented. What and who can compare to this? Yet, he never sacrificed his courage or confidence to be the true light of the world. He was bold, brave, and shrewd as he implemented his "save the world" plan and then allowed himself to be executed when he was ready. Jesus lived community humbly among us never above us.

When I was nine years old, I used to watch my dad jog, and occasionally we would go on jogs together. He would jog so slow that it occurred to me I could beat him. So I challenged him to a race. He grinned his megawatt grin and chuckled a bit as he politely declined.

I pestered him for weeks for a race until he finally agreed. At the time, we lived across the street in the church parsonage, and he told me to meet him after work for the big race.

I looked forward all day as I watched the clock for the moment when I would beat my dad and prematurely relished the celebration in my vivid imagination. When the time came, I put on my running shorts, tank top, and wrist sweat bands. I braided my hair to keep it out of my face while I was flying, double knotted my fastest sneakers, and jogged over to my dad's office for warm up, careful not to wear myself out too much.

When I arrived, Dad was closing his black Samsonite briefcase. He was still in his dress slacks, black leather spit-shined shoes, shirt, and tie, complete with his gold Cross pens secured to his breast shirt pocket.

I gasped, "Aren't you going to change?" He was going to lose big! He quietly picked up his case and gently told me he was fine. Now I was feeling bad for the guy. I told him we could leave the briefcase here and pick it up later. Again, he said he'd just carry it and run. I shook my head as I pictured his slow jogging gait and his awkward briefcase, knowing this would be an easy win for me.

As we got out to the curb, he said I could tell us when to go. He even offered me a head start which I confidently declined. I had this in the bag!

When I hollered "Go!" We both took off running, Dad in his full business gear and briefcase in hand. He ran like I had never seen him run before. I was running for all I was worth, and Dad was putting so much distance between me, it was like I was running in place!

I was too shocked to be humiliated. Dad was very, very fast, and even in his dress attire and briefcase, he ran fast and strong. In a nanosecond, I suddenly realized I could never beat him no matter how fast I ran. He was waaaayyy faster than me. All I had ever seen was him jogging slowly. Looking back, I realized he was always jogging slowly so I could keep up with him. He never took off running at full speed so we could be together and I wouldn't feel inferior to him.

When I got back home, Dad just smiled his playful smile, gave me a knowing look that said, "You get it." I now know why dad refused my repeated invitations to race him. He didn't want me to feel like this—a very slow, less-than-effective runner. He wanted me to believe I was fast, even faster than him so I could do anything I wanted. He didn't want me to be defeated, but he knew there was danger in me thinking I was better than I was.

I learned humility that day but was never humiliated by him. In his win, he didn't gloat or tease me. He respected the moment as a tender learning time for me to see myself more accurately, and to see the proper power of my dad. My humility brought wisdom, as I became wiser to the realities of who I was and who my dad was. After that day, I often wondered how fast my dad could really run.

Unbeknownst to me, Dad played football at Colorado State University and was known for being a fast, tough player with a lot of heart and strength. His nickname was Swivel Hips because of his strength and agility to outrun and outmaneuver the other players.

My nine-year-old self thought I could outrun a college football player based on how he was jogging with me.

This is our God. He is so great, so awesome, and so incredibly fast. The scripture tells us God is light, and light travels 186,000 miles per second. So if God travels as fast as light or faster, we have one very fast God! Yet, he jogs slowly next to us so he can be with us and encourage us to keep going. This is humility. We can easily misunderstand the strength, speed, and heart of God when he becomes *us* to be with us. But do not be fooled. He is an awesome, relational God who chooses to humbly walk with us when he can fly.

Later, as my dad was fading away from a lung disease, I found myself jogging slowly next to him then walking and eventually wheeling him in his wheelchair. He walked slowly and breathing became a difficult and laborious task, and I found myself recounting this story as a child of attempting to race my dad. Now, I could easily outrun him, but I didn't want to. Like him, I enjoyed his presence so much, I adjusted my gait so I could walk with him. I was grateful he taught me how to be humble so I could return the favor.

In Micah 6:8, we are called to love justice and mercy and to walk humbly with our God. Our humble God adjusts his gait for us as he walks, crawls, jogs, and even carries us instead of flying at the speed of light because he so enjoys our presence and desires to be together.

He could race ahead leaving us in the dust to fend for ourselves, while showing off how fast he is. But he doesn't. He lingers, waits, and beckons us to just enjoy his presence. Yet because he loves justice, he will show us when we are too self-exalted in who we are thus provoking harm to ourselves and those around us. But like a loving father, he will be merciful as he reminds us who we are and who he is.

When we walk with him, we become wise. Our world needs more justice and mercy and the wisdom a humble leader brings who is about exalting healthy community versus exalting self. Like anyone we spend time with, we learn how to be influenced by them. When we spend time with a humble God, we learn how to be a humble servant leader, and to become one with those around us as we walk in humility with a just, merciful, humble, wise God.

A Humble Leader

Nelson Mandela spent twenty-seven years in prison as a political prisoner then became president of his country and peacefully abolished apartheid in South Africa. In the fall of 2018, I was able to visit Robben Island where Mandela was imprisoned and the cell in which he spent preparing for the revolution he was destined to lead. Oprah Winfrey described him as one of the most humble people she's ever met. He saw himself as part of a larger force, a regular human who was able to create peaceful transformation in his country because of the efforts of others.

Here's how he wanted to be described: "I wanted to be known as Mandela, a man with witnesses. Especially because I knew it was not the contribution of one individual which would bring about liberation and the peaceful transformation of the country. My first task when I came out was to destroy that myth that I was something other than an ordinary human being." [12] He saw himself as nothing special but just a part of a body that would transform his country.

In his humility, he didn't see himself as weak, ineffective, or inferior, but as a powerful, capable world-changer. Nor did he minimize his feelings from the injustice he experienced or witnessed. He just refocused and made changes that would better his life and the lives of others.

Here are his words when asked how was he able to forgive his oppressors and not become bitter: "Well, I hated oppression, and when I think of the past, and the type of things they did, I feel angry. You have a limited time to stay on this earth. You must try to use that period for the purpose of transforming your country into what you desire it to be. And therefore, you have to reject all negative visions in your own soul, in your blood system, and focus your attention on the positive things." [13]

He was, as one Pinterest quote said, "Humble enough to know I'm far from perfect. Confident enough to know I can do anything I set my mind to." [14]

Humility is not becoming an inferior human but rather a powerful person who partners with and relies on the skills, ability, and passions of others. "Self-pity isn't humility. It's the opposite of humility. It screams for people to look at us and notice how much we've suffered. Humility is the bedrock security that doesn't demand or expect applause or recognition."[15]

Humble people know their limits—their capacity, weaknesses, and strengths—and develop others as they partner with them, integrating their ability and giftedness for the better of the whole. Humility focuses on the positive, the end-goal, and brings everyone along with you to achieve that final goal. "A common misconception is that humility involves having a low self-esteem, a sense of unworthiness, and/or a lack of self-focus. However, true humility involves an accurate self-assessment, recognition of limitations, keeping accomplishments in perspective, and forgetting of the self. Humble people do not distort information to defend or verify their own image, and they do not need to see—or present—themselves as being better than they actually are."[16]

I was able to see this humble leader up close and personal when I visited his memorial museum in Johannesburg. Throughout the displays, Mandela's passion to end the oppression of his people and establish a just and fair community for all was reinforced. Those twenty-seven years of isolation, stillness, and feeling forgotten, unwanted, or unneeded no doubt played a large part in developing the humility necessary to unite his country and abolish the apartheid peacefully.

On May 10, 1994, he went from jailbird to the first president elected of South Africa under the new constitution. Miraculously, he ended apartheid in South Africa with all its horrors in a peaceful revolution and without oppressing the very people who oppressed his people for centuries. His legacy lives on as he continues to inspire his people to respond with mercy, strength, and humility in their leadership when confronting their oppressors and developing the vision for a just, unified country.

Humility with the Earth

Humility is derived from the word *humus*, which means earth and soil.[17] It signifies being grounded or from the earth, which is a beautiful description of humility, as one who has his/ her feet planted firmly on planet earth. When we over-consume our resources and don't care for our earth it is a lack of humility before the world we share with all humankind.

Recently, Jake and I were on a trip to San Diego. We thought it would be fun to bike to the southernmost tip of California where it borders Mexico. We biked to the beach, which had a foul odor and brown waters that smelled and looked very different from the beautiful beaches up north.

As we dismounted our bikes and prepared to walk the white sands, a huge yellow hazard sign warned of the dangers of swimming in toxic waters. Unlike the crowded San Diego beaches up north, this beach was completely vacant. We questioned a local couple about the differences, and they said it was the waste coming from Mexico that was floating onto our beaches. They commented how this has been a problem for years, with little improvement.

There are joint efforts to assist Mexico in properly disposing of their trash, and I wanted to say to the powers that be "Let's work harder together, this just can't be." My heart sank at the unoccupied beaches due to toxic waters. It was at that moment

I realized how tiny our planet is as bodies of water and oceans connect us all. We are dependent on each other, and we must help one another and work humbly together to sustain our great earth.

As we started our trek toward the Mexican border, we noticed areas of beach roped off. A sign greeted us with a child's writing: "Please stay out of this area to preserve." Another sign gave a detailed explanation complete with children's drawings of how important it was to preserve a certain ground covering growing in the beach sands because this provided food and a nesting place for a particular seabird.

As we walked, we saw several more carefully roped-off areas with more vegetation growing, and my heart warmed toward the hands so carefully maintaining the bird life amidst beaches containing toxic waters. They were my heroes, and I found myself wishing to be like them when I grow up.

I wondered at the arrogance I've displayed by treading carelessly across terrains, unaware of the damage I do to the life that depends on it. I wondered at the arrogance of adults who pollute a world only to leave toxic beaches to our children. I wondered at the arrogance of nations unbothered by or incapable of responsibly disposing of their waste.

I checked out the standing our country has with the rest of the world in our environmental performance, and here is what I found:

"The United States places 27th in the 2018 EPI, with strong scores on some issues, such as   Water   & Sanitation (90.92) and Air Quality (97.52), but weak performance on others, including deforestation (8.84) and GHG emissions (45.81). This ranking puts the United   States near the back of the industrialized nations, behind the United Kingdom (6th), Germany (13th), Italy (16th), Japan (20th), Australia (21st) and Canada (25th)."[18]

We are 27th, which isn't bad as compared to the rest of the world but not great as compared to our industrialized neighbor nations.

We can do better. We must do better and humbly respect the limitations of our earth and provide a beautiful legacy for our children. It's rather arrogant to think they should be cleaning up our messes, don't you think?

Reflection:

How are you humble with yourself? Your close relationship? Your work? Your church?

Do we comfort them when they cry or quote scripture at them?

Do we condemn, shame, and judge instead of love, accept, and honor?

When has someone walked next to you when they could be running?

When have you walked next to someone when you wanted to sprint?

How is God walking with you today? How are you walking with him?

What are you doing to express humility for our earth?

What enviornment causes are you involved in to make earth improvements?

Who is wise and understanding among you?
Let them show it by their good life, by deeds done in
the humility that comes from wisdom. (James 3:13)

GENTLENESS

Virtue of Humanity: Gentleness Improves Humanity

"In a gentle way, you can shake the world."

—Mahatma Gandhi

Gentle Teaching with a Gentle God

There is a movement sweeping throughout Canada and beyond called Gentle Teaching. It was designed by John McGee to be used with marginalized people groups, elderly, developmentally delayed, and special needs kids, and it emphasizes relational teaching through mentoring.[19] According to their website they believe: "Every human being longs for a relationship in which he feels safe, loved, loving, and connected. In gentle teaching we call this relationship 'Companionship.'"[20]

This is the basic description:

Gentle Teaching

I teach you to feel safe with me

I teach you to feel loved by me

I teach you to feel loving towards me

I teach you to feel connected with me

Because many are recovering from broken trust and hearts consumed with fear, Gentle Teaching believes people need unconditional love to heal, learn, and develop new skills. Gentle Teaching refers to this as "companionship" and claims creating companionship with vulnerable population groups is especially important since they have significant struggles connecting and feeling love, even with their caretakers. The four pillars are: safe, loved/valued, loving, and engaged.

Safe: Feeling safe is the foundation for building trusting, meaningful relationships; this includes feeling emotionally, physically, psychologically and environmentally safe.

Loved/Valued: Our goal is to create cultures of support where everyone feels valued, regardless of their interactional challenges. Recognizing that behaviors are a symptom of feeling emotionally unsafe, a person does not need to earn our approval. Supporting a person to experience the unconditionally of relationship is essential.

Loving: To truly be a part of community, one must find value in being in relationship with others. It is a caregiver's responsibility to demonstrate the skills necessary to become connected to the people around us, assisting others to nurture meaningful relationships.

Engaged: In order to live fulfilling lives, people need to have purpose in their days. Discovering ways to get involved in meaningful activities, finding value in relationship, and building connections within community is an essential aspect of one's life journey meaningful relationships.[21]

McGee describes Gentle Teaching as the psychology of interdependence, which theorizes that every human being needs to live connected with others in equal and mutual relationships and embedded in a loving and caring community. This community invites the individual to develop his qualities for the benefit of himself/herself and the community. Positive and uplifting teaching is promoted for making changes and developing safety in community.

When I first discovered Gentle Teaching, I found myself longing to be a part of this community. Teaching with gentleness is something we all crave but few have mastered. We long to be valued enough that others connect with us before anything is expected from us. To learn enveloped in love and relationship, deeply connected with an adoring teacher, spouse, or minister. To ask a question knowing it was the perfect question to be asked. To be noticed, reassured, affirmed, and validated throughout the learning process so connection and healing can happen and thus inspire real growth. Not the cheap, synthetic growth with shallow roots that regurgitates what the teacher wants to hear, but the deep, life-altering, character-developing growth that causes us to flourish and propels us to our destiny. Connected, loved, safe, and cocooned in this loving community till we are able to fly on our own. This sounds like Mr. Roger's neighborhood.

Coincidentally, this reflects the heart of our maker. God wants us to know him as a gentle Being, like a whispering blowing breeze that moves gently around, with, and through us. When God wanted Elijah to see him, he told Elijah to go stand in a cave on a mountain and he would pass by. Here's what happened:

> *Then a great and powerful wind tore the mountains*
> *apart and shattered the rocks before the Lord, but*

*the Lord was not in the wind. After the wind there
was an earthquake, but the Lord was not in the
earthquake. After the earthquake came a fire, but
the Lord was not in the fire. And after the fire came
a gentle whisper. When Elijah heard it, he pulled
his cloak over his face and went out and stood at the
mouth of the cave.* (1Kings 19:10-18)

God chose to reveal himself in a gentle breeze instead of powerful winds, an earthquake, or a fire. A gentle, soothing, refreshing breeze. This is how the Creator of the universe decided to introduce himself to Elijah, as if to say, "I'm mighty, but I'm gentle." Like a gentle teacher, he reinforced the Gentle Teaching pillars through the work of Jesus and his ministry on earth. The original author of Gentle Teaching, God is our companion since the garden days and has worked hard to remain so despite our disruptive behavior.

A Gentle Leader

"Gentleness, self-sacrifice and generosity are the exclusive possessions of no one race or religion."
—Mahatma Gandhi

". . . You need a way to continuously in an ongoing manner give unconditionally valuing to this person who is filled with fear. So you talk, you tell stories, you uplift the person, 'you're good.' You don't focus on what the person has done but who they are, mind, body, and spirit. You remember that your purpose is to teach that other, you are my companion, I will help you, you can come with me."[22]

If you haven't witnessed one of these gentle teachers, you are deprived of a beautiful scene. I don't know his name, and I'll probably never meet him again, but I will never forget him. The impact he made on my life was profound. Jake and I were at the movies when we noticed this tall, casually dressed man enter the theater calmly pushing a wheelchair-bound quadriplegic woman to the handicap section. We watched him gently tip her chair back, settle her in with a blanket, and bend down to listen to her whispered requests then make more adjustments with her chair, body, blanket, etc. Confident she was satisfied, he dropped down in the chair beside her.

As the movie began, we found our eyes often drifting down to the scene below us. He'd give her some popcorn, wipe her mouth, give her a sip of pop, then give himself a few bites and sips and resume the routine. Sometimes she would cough, and he'd stoop to lift her head then continue the popcorn/pop regimen.

As he regularly moved to attend to her needs, his movements were easy, familiar, not rushed or impatient, and I wondered how he could watch any of the movie. When they finished their snacks, he held her hand beside her or would slip his arm up around her head, alert to her small cues, then make more adjustments.

It was so moving to watch that, as the credits rolled, Jake couldn't resist approaching the man. He discovered she was his wife and had suffered a spinal injury from a car accident several years ago. With tears in his eyes, Jake thanked the man for being such an inspiration to him for how to gently treat and serve his wife. Without hesitation, the man responded, "I wouldn't have it any other way." A truly gentle teacher and the epitome of a gentleman.

This husband reminded his bride who she was to him by how he cared for her, loved her, and put her needs before his as he operated as a safe and loving companion. The fear she must feel on a daily basis about putting her life in someone else's hands for some of the most menial tasks was daunting. The sadness and depression she must have gone through at being a healthy, walking, running woman to losing the use of all her limbs and confined to a chair for life must have been unbearable, yet here they were. He was teaching her she had value to him for being his companion, lifting her up, taking her to the movies to have popcorn and pop while serving her in this continuous, calm manner. She mattered to him, and it was clear he wanted her for who she was and not for what she could offer. Just another couple in love going to the movies for date night.

What a beautiful way to be mentored. So many times in learning a new job, training involves emotionally distant learning, like learning a policy book, going to trainings, or observing another worker. Abrupt corrections, demeaning remarks, and highlighting mistakes often define the training experience, then are repeated by the now-experienced employee to the new, timid employee.

Recently at a department store, I was being helped by a new trainee and I felt for the woman as her trainer looked on with a critical and menacing look, just daring her to mess up. The trainee felt her presence and became flustered as she was doing the sales transaction, and made several consecutive errors, for which she was roughly criticized by the trainer. After the trainer abruptly corrected her for the third time and apologized to me for her error, she explained demeaningly, "She's in training," while rolling her eyes at me as if she wasn't even there. This is a common scene and experience for people in training, if you are trained at all. Trial and error is a common training technique, then harsh criticism if you mess up. Developing connection, companionship, or a safe experience for learning is rarely a consideration for job training.

When you get frustrated, embarrassed, uncomfortable, and frightened, you think with the smallest part at the back of the brain. It trips our fight, flight, or freeze adrenaline responses making learning very challenging if not impossible as we become bent on surviving. You are literally operating backwards.

As a teacher, I was trained not to teach beyond a child's frustration level because no learning takes place. The front part of the brain or the prefrontal cortex is the largest part of the brain, which needs to be activated in order for learning to happen. When we are relaxed, loved, safe, and connecting in a healthy way, the hormone oxytocin is released, enabling us to relax and feel safe so learning can take place.

Gentle Teaching activates the front part of the brain, keeping the fear, stress, and adrenaline at bay. This allows growth to happen as oxytocin is stimulated, creating a safe haven for our brains to flourish. Love keeps us out of fight, flight, or freeze mode, while fear and shame make us bent on survival.

Our Creator knew this, which is probably why he chose to be seen as a gentle breeze instead of a violent tornado. One provokes fear, while the other stimulates love. Romans 2:4 says, God takes us firmly by the hand and leads us into a radical life-change. It is his kindness that leads us to repent or have a change of heart, so all the more we want to invite change through kindness. We are hard-wired to learn this way and improve humanity through our kindness toward one another. Yet, we cannot give what we do not have, so if we are not being kind to ourselves, we cannot share this with others. Treating ourselves gently makes way for expressing gentleness to others and our beautiful earth.

Gentleness to Our Earth

The organization Gentle Ways for our Planet has the vision "All beings on Planet Earth co-exist and thrive through sustainable collaboration."[23] They believe it takes a concerted effort and intentional living to insure the well-being of all of earth's inhabitants. They promote gentle ways to create thrivability for all species on our planet. It is through compassion for our earth that we respond with actions that foster a gentle environment for endangered species and compromised vegetation to thrive in. Remember the sea bird habitat protection project of local San Diego children? They get it.

Being gentle with one another or our earth when in distress is a beautiful but foreign concept to me. I was raised by parents who came from the generation where conservation, recycling, and earth pollution was not a hot topic in the news coverage. I was also raised where using force to get your children to do things was considered appropriate and "good Christian" parenting. "Spare the rod, spoil the child" and "children should be seen and not heard" were common parenting philosophies of my childhood years.

When I was talking back to my mom, my dad would overhear and playfully start singing "Smack them down again, Maw, smack them down again. We don't want the neighbors talking 'bout our kin." Although provoking, I got the message, and stopped back-talking.

Looking back at this as a parent, I see some of the comic relief this provided for getting me to behave. I also assume the best intent for my parents in wanting well-behaved kids. Also, they were products from their parents' parenting and society's parenting values during their era.

But the message was aggressive and anything but gentle. It taught me to parent in aggression, relate in aggression, and overpower vs. communicate in gentleness to those who have differences. The lack of gentleness instilled fear in me. The fear was manifested in angry outbursts and aggressive communication. Looking back, I think my home could have used more gentleness and love in inspiring good behavior.

Through my own therapy, I had to learn and am still learning how to be gentle with myself so I can be gentle with others and offer gentle responses to my earth. If I allowed myself to harbor any deep regrets, it would be the lack of gentleness I have exhibited to those most dear to me. Similarly, I have completely underestimated the power of gentleness to foster transformation with our environment and all the inhabitants of our beautiful planet.

Gentle people transform relationships and environments through gentleness and are contagious. I believe the best way to foster gentleness is to raise gentle humans. Teaching my children to care for their small tea cup poodle at a young age has created tender adult humans who value life in any form. Our world is hungry for gentle teachers. I think this is the great draw to newfound heroes such as Mr. Rogers and Bob Ross. They sweated gentleness and used their gentle messages to inspire a community revolution. In their own innovative ways, they popularized gentleness, giving it the esteem it deserves.

When Jake wears his Bob Ross socks with happy little clouds, I smile every time.

Reflection:

How are you gentle with yourself? Your close relationship? Your work? Your church?

How does God correct you kindly?

When you mess up, how do you speak to yourself?

What is some Gentle Teaching you can give yourself to grow?

How do you want others to feel when you confront them?

What do you do when others are unkind or harsh with you?

Describe a gentle mentor you've had in your life.

How can you treat our earth with more gentleness? What can you preserve? Protect?

"Feelings are everywhere—be gentle."

—*J. Masai*

PATIENCE

Virtue of Courage: Patience Demands Courage

"Every great dream begins with a dreamer. Always remember, you have within you the strength, the patience, and the passion to reach for the stars to change the world."

—Harriet Tubman

Patience Is Powerful

When I think of patience, I imagine the scene from *Braveheart* where the Scots are lined up in battle with William Wallace waiting for his command as the English army presses down on them. You see his hand raised in battle signaling his army to wait patiently as the English run full force, advancing on his army, which is positioned in a line awaiting their approach. Then, at what appears to be at the last minute, Wallace drops his hand and screams "NOW!" as the Scots all raise their logs hewn into huge spears, shocking the English as they run headlong into them, stabbing them to death.

Okay, that part was a bit gruesome to view, but I loved the patience of the Scottish army as they planned the attack and executed a flawless delivery. Patiently waiting to deliver a well-hatched plan, vision, or calling takes a lot of courage as life's hardships come bearing down on you. But if you move too quickly, then you are at risk of losing everything you've worked hard to develop. We may think we're ready, but God may have other ideas of what we need to develop before we implement the vision and plans he has placed on our hearts.

A Patient Leader

Author and member of UCLA's Psychiatric Clinical Faculty Dr. Judith Orloff describes the kind of patience needed to act powerfully in a *Psychology Today* article: "Patience doesn't mean passivity or resignation, but power. It's an emotionally freeing practice of waiting, watching, and knowing when to act."[24]

The movie *Harriet* chronicles the story of slave-turned-abolitionist Harriet Tubman. Harriet embodied the trait of patience, waiting to seize the moment to act. Patience is not to be misinterpreted as passivity as Harriet waited for the right moment to flee her life of slavery. Harriet prayed for her master to die for blocking her family's freedom and threatening to split them apart. A week later he did, and it was all Harriet needed to plan her escape and act powerfully. Her escape to freedom provided her the opportunity to facilitate the escape from slavery of seventy more people, including her family members. In a ten-year span, she made thirteen more visits to the south to free her people. Her deep faith, ability to hear God's voice, and passion for freedom made her a powerful leader because of her patience and the courage to act at the right time.[25]

Slavery must have broken the heart of God. How many people did he speak to before Harriet? He showed incredible patience in working with a human, a lowly slave girl, who had the courage to act and the patience to listen to his voice. He could have sent angels and a whole army to free his people, but he chose one courageous girl who dedicated her life to the cause.

In order to have patience verses passivity, we need to have passion for a hope that drives us to act when the time is right. Too many times we can become complacent, indifferent, or confused about what really matters because our patience becomes replaced with passivity. Ask yourself: what are you passionate about? What drives you to be better? To make changes? What is the hope calling you to live your purpose each day?

There is a brightly colored picture by artist Kelly Rae Roberts that hangs in my office. It is a woman's face lifted upward, appearing to be listening and looking to a distant presence, which is captioned "What is calling you?" The picture haunts and inspires me to be intentional with what is calling me each day I go to work. On the opposite wall hangs a decorative picture of the Lord's Prayer, which seems to be the answer to this often perplexing question.

I don't know if this is divine design or my subconscious at work, but the two pictures appear to be conversing, one asking while the other answers. For I know my ultimate desire is to bring a bit of heaven to earth every day in how I love, live, and relate with the humans around me, as I attempt to emulate my Creator, the true community maker. Hope inspires us to be patient as we wait with eager but restrained actions to move when the timing is right. It is in patience I continue to write, hoping my words will spark a fiery hope in us to develop safe, loving community.

Relationships require so much hope and patience. Nothing exercises patience more than parenting and marriage. It is here we learn to develop patience if we want and lean into the hopes we have for our children and our marriages. To pray our hopes gives grounds for God and us to move so prayers become realities. Passiveness in the face of the hope we are called to gives grounds for despair, depression, and divorce to take root. When we can we need to have hope to fuel our patience in what will bring out the best in ourselves. Sometimes, patience needs to be exercised in discerning when to leave a marriage or use tough love in our parenting. Patience is always needed in recovering the love, reconnecting to new loves, and developing character in children.

Physician and inspirational writer Dr. Alex Lickerman suggests three ways to develop patience:

1. *Self-confidence that you can win.* When we believe that we can win, we wait expectantly and patiently for the win to happen.

2. *Recognition that your goal isn't crucial for your happiness.* Our sense of urgency can be calmed when we recognize that no goal is critical to our ultimate happiness. As we work diligently to achieve our goal, it is important we remind ourselves of this truth.

3. *A determination to advance one step at a time.* Take one day at a time, doing the tasks for that day and allowing the tasks of tomorrow to be accomplished then. When we do this, we will find ourselves suddenly in front of our goal.[26]

Patience to Our Earth

When biologist Christine Figgener filmed a gruesome video of her team removing a plastic straw from a sea turtle's nose, she didn't expect it to go viral. It was viewed by over

33 million people and started a movement to eliminate plastic straws from our planet and introduce biodegradable straws in large companies around the world. She was just doing her job and decided to film her work so others could watch what she was patiently doing day by day. By letting the general public into her world, they were able to see the problem and respond:

- Large companies like Alaska Airlines, Starbucks, and Disney are phasing out plastic straws
- Cities and states like San Francisco, Seattle, and California are banning the use of plastic straws
- The European Union is moving to decrease and prohibit the use of plastic products

Figgener's life has changed dramatically too as she has found herself uncomfortably straddling academia and the advocacy world. She has become a community activist and a presenter at schools, colleges, and other venues, and is involved in a documentary project.

Time Magazine named Figgener a Next Generation Leader. She has learned that communicating beyond the academic world is valuable but claims she has learned to be constantly vigilant and cautious as to the impact and presentation of her message. As a scientist, she didn't set out to win any beauty pageants or create a world renowned video that thrust her in the spotlight and public life. "Delivering compelling messages is difficult," she says. "I am used to obsessing over my data, not over how I look on camera. My research is dirty and smelly, full of long hours and unkempt hair. Conservation campaigns focus more on appearances, marketing and selling."[27] Yet, she expresses the conflict in abandoning the spotlight so she can study marine life thus decreasing advocacy for the very animals she loves and has dedicated her life to.

Her patience to watch, wait, and take the courage to act has changed our earth and improved conditions for marine life. For my part, I can endure ice clinking on my teeth if it saves a turtle's life or improves the quality of life for our planet's other critters. Thank you, Christine, for the courage, hope, and patience you demonstrate in improving our earth and inspiring others to do the same.

Reflection:

How are you patient with yourself? Your close relationship? Your work? Your church?

How does God show patience to you?

What is calling you?

What do you hope for?

Is there something you are waiting for patiently? Are you waiting for your moment to act courageously?

Describe a patient mentor you've had in your life.

What is your hope for our earth?

When you see our earth and its inhabitants groaning and struggling to survive, are you acting patiently with hope to create new changes? Are you watching and knowing when to act?

What are you doing to express patient care for our earth?

"Have patience with all things but first with yourself."
—Saint Francis de Sales

LOVE

Virtue of Transcendence: Love Transcends Reality

"You know you're in love when you don't want to fall asleep because reality is finally better than your dreams."

—Dr. Seuss

Love Gives Hope

Love truly is needed to express an appreciation of beauty and excellence, gratitude, hope, forgiveness, humor, and playfulness, and to go beyond this reality to another spiritual reality that runs by a whole other set of rules. A place where grace is abundant, justice is attainable, beauty surrounds us, and joy infiltrates us. Where negativity, sadness, shame, rejection, and despair are dismantled as we are lifted to another loving, honoring reality. Like a bird that needs wings to fly, love is the wings that help our hearts take flight over the negativity of this world. It lifts us to another reality where we can fly higher than our bodies ever allow us to. Love gives hope and enables us to have a sense of purpose as we pursue what we desire and love. It is endless and abundant and is the fuel needed to change our lives, relationships, and world.

God is Love

It is impossible to befriend a God we don't love and enjoy or don't feel loved or enjoyed by, and I cannot talk about a loving God without talking about grace. Sometimes when people describe their view of God to me, they often describe him as distant, uncaring, cruel, or indifferent to their plight in life.

One woman felt intense shame for having four abortions throughout her younger years. After carrying this burden for over forty years, she finally confided in me. She hadn't even told her husband of twenty-five years! Knowing she had a faith, I asked her if she talked to God about this.

She vehemently shook her head and said, "I haven't told him yet. I'm too ashamed, and he might not love me."

I told her, "I think he already knows."

She nodded knowingly and said, "I'm just not ready to share this with him because he is too far away."

I reassured her of her decision to not confide in a God that appeared unloving, uncaring, and distant. I told her I wouldn't confide in her God either. Here was the irony I saw so many individuals negotiate: praying and believing in a "God," that doesn't even love them! Together we talked about a loving God she could confide in. A God that would give her grace, love, and relief from the burden she'd been carrying for so long. Her assignment was to discuss her pain with this "new" God. The next session, she came in with a smile the size of Texas and announced, "I am forgiven, and he still loves me." On her ankle was a fresh tattoo that simply said "GRACEFULLY LIVING."

Sometimes as we grow, we have encounters and experiences that mar our understanding of the loving character of God. When I was five, I remember falling asleep talking to my friend. My very best friend, who liked me and loved me enough to want to hang around me all the time. This was God to me. Like a friend, he cared for my hurts, comforted me when I cried, celebrated my successes, and thoroughly enjoyed me.

Through the years, preachers, teachers, authors, and churches, have tried to introduce another God to me. One who is ashamed of me, constantly judging, criticizing, and condemning me. When the FOG (fear, obligation, and guilt) became so thick that discouragement and despair would set in, I would find myself striving for his love instead of relating to him in a loving friendship. Then like a quiet breeze that would gently blow away the fog, I would see my real Friend once again-accepting, caring, and desperately in love with me. God would use his messengers to remind me of his true character. One such messenger came in the form of my middle school teacher, Mr. Chris.

I grew up attending a Christian school with chapel services once a week, and some chapel speakers took it as their personal challenge to convict us. For my sensitive heart, this was never a challenge. One particular chapel service, the speaker delivered a severe message about disrespecting our parents, teachers, and other adults "placed in authority in our lives." He warned me of a God who hated sin and demanded repentance so as to not block his blessing and loving relationship. In my conscientiousness, I remember trying to rack my brain of which adult I had to apologize to for my disrespect. I landed on my science and bible teacher Mr. Christopherson, who we affectionately called Mr. Chris. It was a daily occurrence that Mr. Chris would have to tell me to stop talking and would write my name on the board for being too chatty.

The speaker had instructed us to go and repent to the

adult we had offended. Just thinking of approaching him still gives me sweaty palms today. I don't remember the stumbling, well-rehearsed speech of repentance and asking for forgiveness I gave, but I'll never forget his response. As I looked up at his large six-foot four-inch frame, with a twinkle in his eye and a smile on his face he replied, "Kiddo, you don't have anything to be sorry for."

I was taken aback. I just gave him the coveted opportunity to do what I envisioned most teachers wanted—to drop the hammer on me! It was like he knew the shame I was wracked with, and he accepted me for just being a great kid who got a little chatty. Unbelievable! In that split second, the grace and love he showed me invalidated so many guilt messages that were delivered to me about God. In that moment, I liked Mr. Chris even more, and I liked the God Mr. Chris believed in.

A Loving Leader

Every once in a while, a person comes along who defies everything reasonable and rational as they live with a fierce love that transcends the most desperate of circumstances. Jackie Pullinger is one such woman. In her book *Chasing Dragons*, she details her over thirty-year ministry in the darkest, foulest places in Hong Kong called the Walled City, where heroin addicts, prostitutes, drug pushers, and more were walled in. The poorest and most forgotten people lived in the most desperate ways to just survive. Whole families lived in one-room apartments, plastic tents, and cardboard boxes, eking out a living. In her early twenties, Jackie bought a one-way ticket to Hong Kong as inspired by a dream she'd had to be a missionary to Hong Kong. Since she was a young single woman, her gender, youth, and lack of marital status prevented missionary agencies, educational institutions, or churches from supporting her. With $100 in her pocket, she went to Hong Kong to bring the love of Jesus, believing this would be the very thing they needed to change their lives. She was right. Jackie brought them the love of Jesus by giving her life to the cause of loving them fearlessly and consistently.

Thirty years later, Jackie houses over 300 drug addicts desiring recovery. She has led drug lords, street people, gang members, and many others to understand they are loved by praying for them and being with them in some of their darkest moments. In the fall of 2018, I was privileged to visit the beautiful estate she built in Hong Kong and experienced one of her church services as the recovering opium addicts sang spine-tinging worship songs in Mandarin. It is hard to believe the sprawling recovery center came from such humble beginnings, through the fearless love of one woman. Through prayer, Jackie and her team have healed many from physical ailments, spiritual wounds, and drug addiction. In Jackie's words, here's what her mission boils down to: "What is important is whether we have loved in a real way—not preached in an impassioned way from a pulpit."[28]

There is no greater love than one who gives up her life for another. Jackie left her London home many years ago and continues to live and minister to the forgotten people of Hong Kong's society. Although the addicts and prostitutes still exist, through her efforts, the Walled City no longer does. Her work has been documented in a film, a book, and many articles, and has caught the attention of state leaders and ministry workers worldwide. Her love was active and went well beyond words as she changed a nation just by loving enough to give her life to the great cause of sharing the love of Jesus. Loving leaders sacrifice their lives for a greater cause that will far outlive them, bringing a bit of heaven to earth nostalgic of those original garden days. Love transcends some of the worst circumstances and helps others to transcend their lives.

God is love, light, and life. To discover a God who loves you, wants to connect with you, and desires your welfare is a magical relationship that transcends the trials of life. To believe your partner, spouse, or friend loves and cares for your needs and wants the best for you is critical for the trust building in a relationship. Why would God be any different? We need to believe he is for us, loves us, and wants the very best for us to have any healthy connection with God, others, and our earth. It is important to have a positive and accurate view of God, or we will resist his presence and friendship. To recognize it is the love of God that causes us to transcend to our highest purpose of living will fuel us to live beyond what we can imagine. Loving God through gratitude, praise, and honest conversation is a way to open up the gateway for God to channel his love to us. Like everything else in the character of God, we are called to live in community with him and others. It is a two-way street where we share love with one another, as love begets love.

Sometimes we need to restructure what we've been taught about love. I find it valuable to make some truth statements that remodel my views on love as a new decree for my life.

Here's my love decree:

I am a creature made in love, designed for love, and flourishes in love. I will be committed to choosing loving relationships, loving me when no one else does, and experiencing a loving relationship with a loving God. I will love by expressing gratitude, affirmation, and appreciation. I will love by sacrificing, giving, honoring, requesting, creating, and forgiving. I will allow myself to need and ask for love. I will choose love to fuel my life and guide my purpose and identity. I will live in loving community at home, at work, and in my city. I will love this beautiful earth well. I will protect myself and those I love from unloving relationships and trust myself to care for me when I feel unloved. I believe in love and will choose to live in love always.

Love the Earth

The documentary *The Game Changers* on Netflix challenges viewers to consider the impact on our bodies and planets of consuming so much animal protein. When we consider what our appetites are doing to our world, it is hard to walk away without making some lifestyle changes. Ironically, eating meat was never in God's original plan.

"Then God said, *'I give you every seed-bearing plant on the face of the whole earth and every tree that has fruit with seed in it. They will be yours for food"* (Genesis 1:29). There was no death so therefore, there were no carnivores—even the animals were vegan. *"And to all the beasts of the earth and all the birds in the sky and all the creatures that move along the ground—everything that has the breath of life in it—I give every green plant for food"* (Genesis 1:30).

It wasn't till sin entered the garden that God killed the first animal to clothe Adam and Eve, and thus the "survival of the fittest" game was on as the food chain became established. Hierarchies developed in animals, nature, and humans as each became fearful of losing power and ultimately death. Peaceful living became a thing of the past as nature and the will to survive became paramount. It is through receiving love from God and from one another that we are able to love our earth and override the damning effects of sin. Where we can, we should choose to sacrifice ourselves, desires, and needs to make this earth a better place for us all to live in. Love counters the effects of sin and casts fear out to create harmonious living. As Christ followers, we are to be known by our love. This includes our earth.

I'm not saying we all need to be vegetarians or vegans, we just need to be more aware of what our appetites are doing to our planet. Is our love for food, natural resources, and precious minerals in balance? Or are we over-consuming thus creating a strain on our earth and its other inhabitants? Where there is love, there is rich life.

Here are 101 ways to love our earth. Enjoy!
https://content.lifeisgood.com/ways-help-earth/

Reflection:

How are you loving with yourself? Your close relationship? Your work? Your church?
How has God shown his love for you?
How do you love God? Others? Our earth?

Who has shown grace to you? Love for you?

Where do you have to forgive God? Others?

How does love transcend you to another emotional and/or psychological space?

What is your love decree?

> "One word frees us of all the weight and pain of life: That word is love."
>
> —*Sophocles*

UNITY

Virtue of Justice: Unity Requires Justice

> "Unity is strength. . . when there is teamwork and collaboration, wonderful things can be achieved."
>
> —*Mattie Stepanek*

Just Leaders Create Unity

If there is unity in a body, there must be justice. One woman I will refer to as Shelly worked for a Christian organization. She was a skilled worker, and a dynamic speaker and leader. Yet despite her natural ability, she was young and needed training and mentoring to do her job better. She solicited help from her boss several times, which he ignored, blaming it on his busy schedule.

Because of her heart for ministry, she often volunteered her time, working well beyond her job description assisting with administrative duties along with her leadership responsibilities. Although she was not compensated in pay or titles, she loved her work so she continued giving. She noticed her director was spending resources and time talking with other male colleagues to train and mentor them and taking them to lunch, coffee, and golf outings giving them more time, attention, and resources. Shelly bravely confronted her boss about the inequity, to which he replied: "I cannot provide this mentoring one-on-one because it would dishonor my marriage values, and I follow the Billy Graham rule."

The Billy Graham rule states that two opposite gender people can never spend time alone unless they're married. The rule is often practiced by Protestant Evangelical male leaders. This gives permission for male leaders to exclude female leaders for moral and ethical reasons, making it very difficult for any woman to protest. Although I'm sure it had its place and was well-meaning at one time, it has been abused, misunderstood, and misused to create an unjust system where men are advanced and women are sidelined and marginalized.

Shelly again showed profound courage by addressing the unfairness of this as she pointed out the conundrum this placed her in, never allowing her to advance. After a year of requesting mentoring and training, she was removed from her position because of "poor job performance," as her male colleagues with less education and experience were advanced, paid, and titled around her. This unjust system is slanted toward men and is a too-familiar experience for women in Christian institutions and ministries. Providing equal mentoring, training, and titles expresses fairness, equity, and value to an individual, and should be offered to all employees, regardless of race, gender, or age.

Nothing breaks unity quicker than unjust systems. We see this throughout history in every culture and country. Our country was birthed from the protests of unjust treatment and taxation of the American/English citizens in the Boston Tea Party. In recent history, we see this through the riots in East LA when unjust treatment was delivered by cops to Rodney King, a black motorist. The #metoo movement raised awareness of the unjust sexual mistreatment of women, provoking a flood of community action for righting the unjust actions of powerful men abusing women. Currently, we are experiencing the grief and horror of the tragic death of George Floyd by the hands of police officers in Minneapolis, Minnesota, on May 25, 2020.

Nations have fallen due to the unjust treatment of their citizens, cultures have been reformed, and religions recreated when justice is absent, breaking unity for the people group. When I was in Zimbabwe in the fall of 2018, the economy was so inflated they were selling their own dead currency to tourists. We bought 50 billion Zimbabwean dollars for one US dollar! When we talked with the citizens, the regular complaint was the corrupt leadership and selfishness of President Mugabe. They repeatedly communicated how he doesn't serve the people by providing basic needs like education, a stable economy, and jobs. He just takes care of himself and his family. His wife Grace Mugabe was so lavish in her lifestyle she has been nicknamed Gucci Grace. While their country struggled to establish education for their children, develop a stable economy, and provide food and work for their people, the Mugabe family was busy collecting their own assets and established a $1 billion net worth that is still being assessed since Mugabe's death shortly after my visit.

In contrast, one of my favorite encounters with a leader attempting to create justice through all the country's chaos was in a downtown street market of Victoria Falls, Zimbabwe. He had no idea what I did but he knew I was traveling for my leadership program. He proceeded to tell me about his leadership dreams and how his nation is in peril because of how poorly they treat their women. So in response to this, aside from running the downtown markets, he also runs "HeShe" classes where he teaches men how to treat women and empowers women to be strong and independent.

He is appropriately named Trymore and was also an artist. He painted a picture of women standing closely together resembling a spine and the babies they carried on their backs were the men to be. He describes women as the backbone of his nation and something for men to protect as they give life to men and their nation. It hangs proudly in my dining room. I told him about my nonprofit women's movement NuShu Sisters, to which he passionately responded, "We need to bring NuShu Sisters to Zimbabwe." Maybe Trymore...maybe. His passion continues to inspire me to seek justice for the sake of unity.

To have a just system, you need a just leader. One who values equity, hears the complaints of injustice and corrects it, and seeks the welfare of others above him/herself. When people are led unfairly, they act unfairly, and unity becomes impossible. Conversely, when leaders lead with fairness, the ground is tilled for unity to be planted, take root, and blossom.

Here's what God has to say about justice:

But you must return to your God, maintain love and justice, and wait for your God always.
(Hosea 12:6)

When justice is done, it brings joy to the righteous but terror to evildoers. (Proverbs 21:15)

But let justice roll on like a river, righteousness like a never-failing stream! (Amos 5:24)

He has shown you, O mortal, what is good. And what does the Lord require of you? To act justly and to love mercy and to walk humbly with your God.
(Micah 6:8)

"Do not pervert justice; do not show partiality to the poor or favoritism to the great, but judge your neighbor fairly." (Leviticus 19:15)

The Lord loves righteousness and justice; the earth is full of his unfailing love. (Psalm 33:5)

Suffice it to say God values and loves justice. If justice is lacking in our relationships and communities, the blessing of unity will be missing. Creating a culture of equity is just and brings joy to the heart of God.

A Leader who Brings Unity

Equitable workplaces where all, regardless of ethnicity, gender, or class, can have equal opportunity for advancement are just. An established, just system of partnering is critical for the health of the individuals and the marriage. A "power-with" partnership instead of a "power-over" hierarchical culture is needed so the couple or organization can work collaboratively to create a just system. This ideal of garden living is rarely achieved without some sort of accountability, which is often accomplished with quotas. Canadian Prime Minister Justin Trudeau is doing just that. He has raised praise and interest for appointing Canada's first cabinet with ethnic diversity as well as developing a gender balance in leadership of men and women, with fifteen each.[29]

The diverse cabinet includes two aboriginal members and three Sikh politicians. When questioned about his intentional diversity, he replied, "It's important to be here before you today to present to Canada a cabinet that looks like Canada." He modeled cultural awareness of his era when he was questioned about his gender-balanced decision by replying, "Because, it's 2015." At forty-three years of age, he is the second youngest prime minister to take office and despite his youth is a leader who gets what it takes to develop unity—embracing diversity. He intentionally brought a cabinet together that balances out the power and shares the decision-making with equal representation. He has joined the gender equality movement introduced to the UN, HeForShe, and is vocal about empowering women worldwide.[30]

Organizations, families, and nations led by leaders skilled at creating unity experience a nurturing, safe culture where they are valued as individuals and equipped to live their best lives as they meet the goals of the community. Sounds like a little piece of paradise we would all want to have.

Unity for Earth Care

It would be a beautiful thing to unify together as inhabitants on the same planet to raise funds, pass laws, and collaborate together to care for its resources. Despite the differences one may have with rapper Lil Dicky and his edgy lyrics, it is quite admirable he pulled thirty celebrities and musicians to perform his charitable musical single "We Love the Earth." It was released in April of 2019 and all the proceeds go to caring for our planet. This collaborative work is an inspiring example of providing unity for a cause we all believe in. It echoes the 1985 charity song by Michael Jackson and Lionel Richie, "We are the World," where over forty musicians and artists came together to record the hit. If musicians and artists can come harmoniously together for a common cause, how much more can faith-based people come together to create a new Eden? Healing our earth is a reasonable, just goal for all people and faith groups to collaborate on and in doing so, creates a sense of unity.

Reflection:

How are you unity-minded with yourself? Your close relationship? Your work? Your church?

When have you experienced unity?

What are some examples of unified communities?

Where do you need to practice living in unity?

Who and what inspires unity for you?

When have you experienced injustice? Justice?

How do you want to collaborate with others to care for our earth?

> "Unity, to be real, must stand the severest strain without breaking."
>
> **—*Mahatma Gandhi***

PEACE

Virtue of Temperance: Peace Requires Moderation

> "Peace is the beauty of life. It is sunshine. It is the smile of a child, the love of a mother, the joy of a father, the togetherness of a family. It is the advancement of man, the victory of a just cause, the triumph of truth."
>
> **—*Menachem Begin***

God Gives Peace through Chaos

A year before I entered my DMin program, my cherished father suffered a death I wouldn't wish on anyone. He suffered from a rare lung disease, Idiopathic Pulmonary Fibrosis. The lungs crystalized and hardened, as he painfully and slowly suffocated to death. Toward his last days, the anxiety became intense and I saw my God-fearing father, who had prayed over and healed many, cry out and shake in terror over the physical and emotional suffering. Although we prayed for healing many times, that was not to be. As I watched my father's body deteriorate, his brain and spirit stayed securely intact, and we both knew this was to be his fate. This man who taught me to love God as a close friend was dying a gruesome death, which highlighted the obvious issue stated by many: when God is close, and is so powerful and loving, there is never an easy or rational explanation why he doesn't heal, protect, or deliver.

Due to his deteriorating lungs, Dad would have violent coughing fits that threatened to consume him, and he appeared to cough up what remaining lungs he had left. I found myself breathing deeply, willing his lungs to fill with the precious oxygen. At one point, the anxiety overtook him, and he lost his ability to emotionally regulate. My fearless, faith-filled father expressed panic beyond words as he shook, cried, and pleaded for help. I helped him to breathe slowly as I encouraged him to refocus and soothe his worries. This is one of the last memories of Dad. He died three weeks later, and I marvel at the peace and temperance we each expressed to get through these dark days.

I'll probably never know why God allowed this death for him on this side of heaven, but I don't really care. All I know is I depended on God's strength to get me through and to grieve the greatest loss I've ever known. My prayers shifted from those of healing to those of dependency as I relied on God's friendship to help me through this dark valley of death. Although I was distraught over the suffering of my dad, we both leaned heavily on the friendship of God and each other to guide us through what should have been very despairing days. Instead, my time with him was often punctuated with silliness as I wheeled him on walks in his wheel chair over bumpy roads, with him pretending to be Darth Vader's voice as we rolled along. Or blasting worship music as we strolled, oblivious to the stares of neighbors as we sang and enjoyed the presence of God. It was a sacred time, and God was with us through the tears, the smiles, and the fears. In the midst of the storm, God granted us a peace that passes all understanding.

Waiting for him to pass over required much patience as we were at the mercy of death's arrival. For us, death was like an unwelcome house guest that does not come when you want and overstays its welcome as it takes its sweet time departing. It hovers around you, threatening to consume at a moment's notice. To stay the course of daily activities amidst intense sorrow and sheer terror demanded the spiritual value of peace. A peace that passed all understanding. I could not have cared for him and gone through my life's greatest sorrows without the beautiful, undeniable presence of peace.

Embracing the Pain Brings Peace

So many times we want to dance around life waiting for the great banquet without having to go through the difficult times or the dark valleys, thinking this will bring more peace. We can't feel happy, fulfilled, and content all the time, despite how much we subconsciously hope for continual happiness. Pain, death, and sadness all have their turn with each of us, and some more than others. One of my favorite visuals of this is Psalm 23. This is how I read it:

The Lord is my shepherd, I shall not want. *(sounds like this is off to a great start!)*
He leads me to lie down in green pastures and leads me by the still waters. *(Hawaii?? Sign me up!)*
He restores me soul *(ahh, now we're talking!)*
Yea though I walk through the valley of the shadow of death *(Huh? Wait just a gosh darn minute!! What happened to the green pastures and still waters?)*
I will fear no evil *(good luck with that! It's like living a real-live thriller movie, and promising to skip peacefully through a house of horrors)*
Thy rod and thy staff they comfort me *(I want more than a rod and staff in the dark valley. An AK-47 maybe? Couple of grenades and sticks of dynamite, please?)*
Thou preparest a table before me *(now we're talkin'!)*
in the presence of my enemies *(not sure if I really want them there but I guess their envy of my good fortune is kind of nice)*
You anoint my head with oil *(Ahh, royalty! I made it! It's safe to assume a crown is coming!)*
My cup runneth over *(Wow, I have more blessings than I can contain!)*
Surely goodness and mercy will follow me all the days of my life. . . *(Lots of good chasing me down. . .forever)*[31]

Too many times we want to stay in the green pastures and by the streams of life, and we dance around the dark valley of death not even wanting to enter, thinking we'll have more peace. We'll do anything not to feel those horrible feelings or avoid challenging circumstances. Can't say I blame anyone. Who in their right mind would choose to go into the dark recesses of your heart and feel the deep pain or be excited to experience a grueling circumstance? The only way I would choose it is if there was going to be a significant payoff. Like eating your vegetables and getting healthy or training for a race to win first prize.

If I could get more peace from not feeling difficult emotions, believe me, I would. But I have found accepting the difficult, painful emotions and experiences is like taking a bitter-tasting medicine that only washes down easier when you have the hope of better days ahead. The sooner you embrace the pain, the sooner you will begin to heal and have real peace. Delaying the difficult emotions through indulgent behavior only delays your healing process. And I don't know about you, but I want to get to that feast as quick as I can, complete with my envious enemies, abundant living, and a greasy head fitted for royalty. We won't be able to avoid those dark valleys, but we can use the peace of God to navigate the darkest of days, knowing peacefulness awaits us.

Peaceful Leaders Have Integrity

Temperance can also be synonymous with moderation. If we want peace, we need to live with moderation and integrity as we align our beliefs with our behaviors. This brings personal peace, which can also provide peace for marriages and communities.

When we live by our values, we bring peace into relationships and into our organizations. I'm sure we are all tragically touched of the moral failings of a leader who had an affair, embezzled funds, or mismanaged work time. I could tell you a story or two, but I'm sure you've heard them. When we say one thing and do another, we create internal and external chaos that affects the harmony and peace of any marriage, relationship, or organization. The trust becomes broken as integrity is questioned, and fear robs us of the peace.

Many times in working with marriages where there is undisclosed infidelity, the other partner can feel a shift in the relationship. Anxiety and fear replace peace and love as the marriage becomes disharmonious. This creates instability in the marriage, and although there is deep sadness when the truth of the affair is revealed, there is also a bit of relief as the reason for their lack of peace is validated. Truth truly does bring freedom, even if it's ugly. Our emotional and mental stability comes when what we say matches what we do. I call this B & B Buddies— the beliefs and behaviors have to be aligned to create good mental health and stability.

Whenever there is instability in an organization or marriage, I look for what is misaligned with the beliefs and behaviors. In order to achieve stability I suggest people change their beliefs or change their behavior in order to align and create stability. For instance, if you believe having affairs is a

valued way to live, you will have better stability for yourself
and the relationship when you do have affairs. If you believe
it is an immoral way to live and do this, then affairs bring
instability. Rarely do people desire to change their beliefs, but
rather they usually opt to change their behavior. This becomes
especially challenging when addictions or a life of indulgence
is present.

Where there is little moderation or temperance, there
is limited peace. I had the privilege of facilitating a women's
group for sexual addiction. It wasn't until they dealt with the
painful sexual and relationship experiences of their past that
they were able to heal. Their indulgence with their addiction
was distracting them from connecting with themselves, God,
and each other. Sound familiar? Food, social media, alcohol,
and work are more socially acceptable addictions but have the
same disconnecting effect. Through caring and sharing, they
were able to enter recovery from their addiction and connect in
a healthy way in their relationships. Temperance keeps us out
of indulgent living and addictions, providing lives of harmony.
When we operate with low temperance, we lose the integrity to
operate with aligned beliefs and behaviors, and we enter into
chaotic living. Choosing temperance in our lives cultivates a
fertile soil for peace to grow in.

Peaceful Earth

One of the biggest take-aways from my studies and
travels in my doctoral leadership program was that our earth
is groaning from the weight of indulgent living. Consumerism

has taken a big toll on the health of human lives and earth's natural resources. In my travels to Thailand, I was deeply saddened by the lack of peace I witnessed as indulgent living demanded the unthinkable from children by greedy, lustful Western men.

In Cape Town, I grieved at the drought that forced locals to adhere to strict daily water rations as tourists consumed more water in a single shower. In Johannesburg, I walked through museums and neighborhoods screaming the atrocities of a greedy apartheid. In Zimbabwe I witnessed the broken economy caused by feeding the indulged whims of their self-absorbed leaders instead of providing education or basic needs for their citizens. In Hong Kong, I was shocked at the low-paid service women who lined the sidewalks every Sunday sitting or lying on sheets of cardboard for their day off because they had no other place to go.

Yet, in all of these places, I met people, leaders, and organizations who were working to make their country a better, more peaceful place as they were choosing a life of integrity lined with temperance. They inspired me to take better care of my earth, its resources, and its inhabitants by living in moderation. I believe we all would like peace on earth. Curbing our indulgences while living with temperance is a great start to creating a peaceful earth.

Reflection:

How are you peaceful with yourself? Your close relationship? Your work? Your church?

How and when have you experienced the most peace?

What are some beliefs and behavior that are aligned in your life? Misaligned?

Where do you need to practice temperance or moderation?

When have you experienced peace in the midst of chaos?

How do you create chaos by not operating in temperance?

How can you provide peace to our earth?

> "It isn't enough to talk about peace. One must believe in it. And it isn't enough to believe in it. One must work at it."
>
> **—Eleanor Roosevelt**

If Adam and Eve were going to church, we would have to address character development so they could make good choices in leading and loving together. We would have to use strategic teaching and classes to alter their character that had transitioned from perfect to self-serving. We would have to reassure them they have to fight the urge to survive and seek the instinctual way of serving. They would need to be reminded that they were made to give and nurture life. They would long for the beauty of living in a garden devoid of fear and saturated in love. They would need to be reassured and comforted with a hope that they can and must be intentional about creating a loving space within themselves and their relationship so they could spread this to their family and beyond. It would be restated that this works best when both of them are being intentional about recreating their garden days they once took for granted. Most of all, they would need to be reminded that perfect love would be the ultimate antidote to the devastating effects of fear.

Keeping in community with their perfect, loving Creator would be the key to their success in recovering their fallen character and creating a church saturated in loving relationships and intentional about giving hope and strategies in developing community-worthy character. When healthy character is developed, we are providing Peer Cultures for our Peer Marriages and Peer Churches to flourish with oneness, echoing the garden living of yesteryear.

COMPLETE | EDEN LIVING

Adam and Eve are living their full paradise once again as they walk in complete authenticity of the perfection with which they were designed. In a perfect world with perfect people. The ultimate garden days are back forever for them. . . and so it will we for us one day. But for now, we are attempting to reclaim Eden in a fallen world in our relationships and our communities. Through the power and relationship of a triune God, we are able to retrieve our garden days even if in small, brief glimpses.

We have the opportunity to choose our eternal destiny and our current earthly destiny. We have been empowered to choose a life of love and power through the work of Jesus Christ, to bring a bit of heaven to earth as we pray the ultimate prayer of community, The Lord's Prayer. He is the father of all, and we are called to worship him in spirit and truth, together, bringing the garden days into being once again. Eden is being reclaimed in our relationships, marriages, and our churches.

CHAPTER 11

Change Strategies

When we consider shaping church culture and shifting it to a Peer Church ethos, we need to commit to change, value mutuality, develop a new language, mentor, be inclusive, provide healing for men and women, and develop a collaborative culture of love.

Shifting from patriarchalism to mutuality in the church demands a commitment by both genders to embrace new alternatives and to develop an increased awareness of the patriarchal culture embedded in societal and religious teachings. In order to change culture, new culture needs to be created. Developing a new culture requires imagination and creativity so new ideas can influence and inspire the existing culture to evolve.

With new changes, resistance can be expected but "profound changes in culture typically take place over the course of multiple generations."[1] In Hebrews 11, we are reminded of all those who have gone before us to carry the torch in establishing Christianity. Despite what God promised, many perished horrible deaths before they were able to receive his promises or experience the religious freedom they hoped for. We experience the freedom today from the men and women who fought for our American rights and died before they could experience the freedoms they bravely fought for. Similarly, Martin Luther King died before he could see his dream lived out for a nation of more equity. This is extraordinary faith— to give our lives knowing we may never fully experience what was promised us or what we envision. A commitment to change requires insight, hope, sacrifice, and faith. What we are committed to changing in our homes and churches today will overflow to the generations beyond.

In developing mutuality, we need to value and listen to each gender's opinions and ask God to inspire solutions for equitable relationships. Knowledge gained is ineffective and unsubstantial if we do not utilize the input of all participants. At a question-and-answer technology event in Saudi Arabia, Bill Gates was asked how Saudi Arabia could be in the top ten countries technologically, to which Gates replied, "Well, if you're not fully utilizing half the talent in the country, you're not going to get too close to the top ten."[2] Similarly, in the church, the integrity structure of the institution is compromised and solutions suppressed when only half of the voices are represented. Both genders must be equally represented in leadership to create a culture of equity and respect.

In every culture, a new language is needed to communicate the vision for imagined changes. Famous theorist Carl Jung believed each person carried both the masculine and feminine within themselves. Without compromising the personality or gender of a person, we need to nurture the femininity and masculinity in each person, allowing individuals to develop their whole selves. Ineffective, outdated teachings can be replaced with the new language of egalitarian teachings for marriages and church leadership.

With leadership development, "Hybrid Leaders," defined as having both female and male characteristics, can be taught and encouraged, expressing value of both genders and countering gender bias.[3] Learning how to speak a language that fosters unity and mutuality rather than division and competition between the genders requires creativity and unconventional thinking.

Statistically, girls stay home more and give back to their communities by developing relationships and fostering healthy changes.[4] Girls and women are literally and figuratively life givers. They birth life to families and church communities, and if we are excluding or silencing women, society and communities are missing out on the life and vibrance femininity brings. An obvious and viable answer to improving our culture and giving new life to communities is to educate and empower females around the globe.

Mentoring and trainings for the girls and women is needed to ignite these changes. A Harvard study researched why men are promoted over women, and they discovered a lack of female mentoring to be a main contributor.[5] In addition, male pastors can benefit from female mentors if they are intent on utilizing more women leaders and closing the gender gap in their churches. Mentoring is essential if a system is to influence the next generation to grow in a healthy and progressive manner without repeating the mistakes of the past.

Inviting one another to develop a gender-inclusive environment, and conversation encourages progressiveness. Those in power need to invite women to be a part of leadership teams and discussions to implement healthy changes. When including women, invite women into discussions by asking them their thoughts and opinions. According to research, women are more apt to participate when invited, and unlike men, they are less likely to self-promote or include themselves.[6]

Research reveals male leaders influence men best, so when they are intentional about mentoring or inviting women, other male leaders are more likely to emulate them.[7] My husband, Jake, is all too aware of this and did his dissertation on men promoting women. He created the website GenderSynergy. us to start conversations for men desiring to use their societal positioning to elevate and help advance women. Male church leaders can have a powerful impact in creating gender-balanced leadership and cultivating an environment of equity, but they must be intentional about advancing women and understand the different leadership styles of women.

Men also need healing from the psychological patriarchy that has limited and defined them unfairly. They need to recover all their emotions as they unabashedly discover and deliver their authentic selves. Building up shame resilience will empower them to take this recovery journey as they share their vulnerable emotions in a compassionate environment. Both genders require compassionate healing from the negative effects of patriarchalism as the wounds run deep in masking the authenticity of each gender. Offering ministry programs or groups addressing this historically controversial issue of patriarchalism in the church would be revolutionary.

Women need healing from the hurts of not being validated in church before they can lead effectively. In order to strategically advance and empower women leaders and equity, here's a plan and shared language we can all echo when the opportunity presents itself. This will address the subconscious as we all individually share the same simple, concrete message to leaders in power.

Develop and Affirm Women Leaders by:

HEARING by validating and accepting their truth instead of invalidating, countering, denying, interrupting, ignoring. . . emotional manipulation or covert abuse.

HELPING by advancing, mentoring, providing fair trainings, support, experts for women and girls of all ages.

HONORING by representing and highlighting women leaders, authors, and speakers, hiring women directors in leadership, and understanding differences.

To accomplish this,
- Develop an objective measuring system to assess and develop gender-balanced leadership.
- Establish a team of leaders who can assess and

develop a healthy integration of gender equity and become leading examples to universities, churches, and societies in how to lead well together.

- Teach healthy character that fosters good community. Have classes taught by coaches and therapists skilled in developing healthy character and thriving relationships, and assist in educating the community.
- Have outside experts provide input and another perspective of the community health.
- Provide a way for community members to voice concerns constructively and confidentially.

In my personal life and in observing the lives of my clients, I can see that change takes time, but God moves quickly, oh so quickly. When we can be open to the work of the triune God in our lives and relationships, God moves quicker than I can keep up with. What an adventure it is with him. I often picture myself hanging excitedly on the back of a roller coaster with my feet flapping wildly and freely behind me as God is playfully hollering over his shoulder, "Keep up!"

It is us humans that slow down the miraculous changes our Eden Maker is wanting to partner enthusiastically with us in. We need to learn to keep up with the Creator who just spoke our universe into being. Then imagine a world beyond what we are living, in our homes and churches, and have the faith to create it joyfully and lovingly with him. When we complete our roller coaster ride, I picture myself breathless with excitement turning to my Divine Adventure Companion and uttering with sheer exhilaration, "What a ride! What's next?" With a twinkle in his eye, I hear him saying, "Hang on!"

CHAPTER 12

Collaborative Culture of Love

Living collaboratively requires cultivating a boisterous culture of love so loud it drowns out the pesky voice of fear. It's as if we are on the edge of Eden threatening to teeter in towards a lush garden of love or outward to the desolate desert of fear. In our desperation to regulate the conflict and order the chaos we establish hierarchies. Author Andrew Marin proposes establishing a collaborative ethos by eliminating hierarchies. He simply states: "No relationship can be built on fear, and true relationships do not have a hierarchy; so don't create one."[1] Scripture confirms the polarization of love and fear: "But perfect love drives out fear" (1 John 4:18). Fear shuts down communication, making collaboration impossible, but love opens up communication and stimulates collaboration.

Providing open forums to discuss thoughts, ideas, and doubts, and pose difficult questions would be a step forward in developing authentic community. Scripture speaks to the early church's defining characteristic believers by describing how they were known for their love (John 13:35), which was displayed through a collaborative culture as they "had everything in common" (Acts 2:44). Conflict, discrimination, church splits, or spiritual abuse is not to be the identifying characteristic of Christianity, but rather a culture of love as evidenced through compassion, grace, truth, generosity, and the fruits of the Holy Spirit (Galatians 5:22-23). Collaborative connections in church are essential in fostering a culture of love and equity.

Ultimately, both sides must step up to create a new culture in marriage and the church that honors the genders in respect to God and the gospel. Assuredly "as long as there is a Holy Spirit, there is hope that we can make strides toward becoming the alliance God created us to be."[2] We all need to be open and committed to healing and change, and intentional about reclaiming Eden.

Without love, we would be doomed. Love covers a multitude of sins, is synonymous with God, and restores all things. Through love, God sent his only son Jesus Christ to restore all things to him and most importantly reverse the devastating effects of sin. Love has a sparkling tone, a beautiful melody, and plays in harmony with loving individuals, communities, and churches singing its tune. When we keep playing the flat, dull, sharp noise of fear, we divide once again, and love cannot be heard or played to have its transforming power on relationships once again. We have to be committed to love—singing, practicing, and playing it confidently for all to experience, hear, and join in with us. Love unites, while fear divides. Just talking about, focusing on, and connecting on fear, divides. Spending as little time as possible on this topic allows love to take front and center stage to do her beautiful, breath-stopping performance.

Through love, Jesus Christ came to restore our world and make all things new, give us abundant life, reunify us to the Father, and rebuild our world from the effects of sin. His seemingly insane master plan was to first become one of us so we could relate to him. Secondly, he conquered the ultimate effect of sin, death, which he strategically accomplished by orchestrating his own personal, gruesome death on the cross. Thirdly, he built a body and group of people to live on after his departure called the Church. This is lived out in smaller community, marriage, and in larger communities of all types of people groups. He gave them strict instructions to love each other, build each other up, and bring others to him. This was dramatically displayed by God's first act on earth after Jesus' death by tearing the curtain in the temple of the Holy of Holies from the top down.

This was a very clear message that the language and culture of sin no longer dominated as he immediately restored us to relationship with himself and each other. He designed the church to be his ultimate tool to overcome evil that not even the gates of hell could stand against, and develop a community of people who lived, breathed, and ministered in the language and culture of love. Fourthly, he left his spirit with us to guide, empower, unify, and heal our broken world from the devastating effects of sin and death. Finally, he left to create a perfect home for us where there will be no more pain, tears, sickness, death, or shame, and where oneness will be had for all eternity. Basically, the ultimate redemption—we get back to the very beginning, the way he designed it to be, new and improved. Eden recreated.

When we choose to live, breathe, and minister under the effects of shame and fear, we are bringing division at every turn and cultivating a breeding ground for chaos and disaster to be harvested. Love cultivates a fertile soil where relationships can be restored, and hope can renew broken relationships and replenish the faith needed to move mountains. We are made for more, for perfection, and to live harmoniously in love. Through the reversing effects of the cross, we now have a choice to move in an upward spiral that takes us closer to our Creator and embodies his redemptive work. Or we can continue in the downward spiral initiated by the crippling effects of fear, shame, and death. Bringing some heaven to earth sounds much more appealing to me as I choose to focus and cultivate the transforming language of love in my life and share with the lives of others I encounter.

The church isn't heaven, but it is designed to be the intermediate space where we get to experience a little bit of heaven on earth, if and only if we choose to speak and live love. A place where we love God, ourselves, each other, and our earth, and live in harmony and equity. And remember, our marriages are mini-churches. What we are called to live in our churches to create oneness also works when applied to our marriages. If we are not experiencing a loving community in the church or in our homes, we may want to question our purpose. The church needs to be the leading exemplar in developing unity and harmony among the genders. And we as Christians need to live a life of inspirational, fearless, sin-shattering love. Anything less does not embody the heart and mind of our God, who is the ultimate embodiment of love.

Couples in Peer Marriages are figuring out how to navigate cultural changes, shifting family dynamics, and live with equity. The church culture can learn much from these marriages who are learning to forge deep friendships, partner equitably, and lead with love. Perceiving a symbiotic relationship between marriages and churches and their interdependency would be valuable for both institutions to acknowledge.

Contemporary Peer marriages can create positive shifts within churches by voicing their concerns, confusion, and desires for more egalitarian leadership and principles to be modeled within churches. Addressing the counter-cultural beliefs of women stand in stark contrast to what the New Testament church originally promoted about women.

As author of *Mixed Ministry* Sue Edwards proclaims, "One thing we know for sure is that our Father calls us to work together in unity not uniformity, respecting and loving each other, complementing one another's individual strengths and weaknesses for his glory and work on earth."[3] It is time for men and women to come together and operate in our giftedness as God has ordained us, instead of operating exclusively according to gender.

Unfortunately, many churches and marriages are struggling with how to make this dream a reality. A prayer for churches would be to experience godly sorrow from the loss the whole body is experiencing that compromises the effectiveness of the gospel. And that this sorrow would lead to a salvation, a new way of living, and would induce change and provoke a justice response for those living without equity. In turn, the psychological sadness of the loss of women and unity between the genders will be healed. A prayer for marriages is to develop healthy character that would lead to unity and oneness in the home and be indoctrinated in churches, and that we find teachers and resources that promote a powerful partnership reminiscent of the garden days. We need each other to be healthy and empowered because God made us to be better together, so through him we can rule and heal our wounded world in love, power, and unity. This is the harmonious melody of mutuality, where Eden is reclaimed.

Jake and I are going on twenty-seven years of marriage. We have just launched our two kids, helped plant a Peer Church and are continuing to learn how to nurture our Peer Marriage as empty nesters. At age fifty, we are different from the young college kids who came together many years ago, yet our passion remains the same—to inspire unity and equity between men and women. Our purpose was developed through our life experiences, our evolving marriage, and over twenty years of therapy work with men, women, and couples. Recently, we both experienced a renewed passion for developing gender parity after completing the Doctor of Leadership program through Portland Seminary.

The spark that started at a young age has only grown stronger as we find ourselves advocating for equity, unity, and love between the genders, and learning to live it with each other.

Jake continues doing counseling for couples and individuals as well as corporate coaching for organizations. I teach leadership classes, give presentations, and together we lead Peer Marriage workshops with our online couples series, One Kingdom. We are currently developing leadership coaching for corporations we contract with desiring healthy Peer Cultures and effective leadership. We find ourselves inspired to assist and attend churches longing to have a Peer Church. Through our therapy work, we are still honored to hear the sacred stories of our clients and encourage ways for people to find harmony in their lives and relationships.

Ultimately, we find ourselves continually learning how to develop better character so we can be better together. Somedays we feel far from Eden as we get lost in our fears of what was instead of nurturing the love of what is. And the differences seem far more glaring than the similarities as we vie for control and participate in childish power struggles in the relationship. Other days we wonder how we could ever stray from Eden and leave the comfort of each other's embrace while living harmoniously in sync with each other. To be truthful, garden living and reclaiming Eden is a conscious choice we each make to love, apologize, forgive, and live with gratitude and authenticity. None of this would be possible without connecting with the master gardener who created the intended paradise we were supposed to live in. Reclaiming Eden is the moments where peace and harmony exist in loving community with God, ourselves, others, and our earth. Having this sustained for eternity is called Heaven, our final home.

Personally, the greatest discovery for me in writing this book is discovering how intricately I am created, how deeply loved I am, and how underdeveloped my character is for having unified community. I am used to doing things on my own and being a helper to others. But to live in community successfully in marriage and the church has led me to develop the spiritual discipline of solitude. Each morning I commit to spending time with my Creator and enlisting his help in developing healthy character fit for garden living. For the first time in my career and life, I have committed a year to myself in developing me. It has been my sabbatical year in allowing space and time for God to develop in me what is lacking.

I am not looking to the validation or affirmation of others to become the woman God has designed me to be. I am looking to God each day to speak to me and reveal what it is he is longing to grow in me. I am journaling and asking myself tough questions like who am I as a mother, wife, sister and daughter? How do I treat myself? How do I love? Who have I not forgiven? What are my boundaries? Who gets my heart? Why don't I ask for my needs? How do I speak the truth in love? How do I respond in love? Am I enough? How do I forgive? Who wants to develop better character so I can be in community with them?

Daily, I find inspiration through the words of Jesus and others as I read, listen, and journal my inner world. I practice, meditate, and consider the six spiritual values, and I wonder how it would look for me to be living those consistently. I find myself struggling the most with patience to wait courageously and hopefully for a newly remodeled, refreshing outcome of me. Then in my wrestling, I find myself impatient and harsh as I realize how little work I've done on developing gentle responses in my life toward me, my beloved Jake, and my family. I am discovering the beauty of my personality and of others through an Enneagram class I attend weekly. I am learning how to express appreciation instead of criticism for the differences of those around me.

Out of care for my earth and my health, I have been vegan for several months now and I'm enjoying the results. It feels gentler to my aging digestive system and to the animal life around me. I run and go on long walks often as I listen to the latest Ted Talk, self-help book, or my worship music playlist.

During this solitude, I have longed deeply for authentic, real connections to help create a safe place to further develop my character. I found it in a mastermind group where we meet once a month to discuss our thoughts, loves, dreams, fears, and aspirations. There are six of us all working together to develop better character and to choose love to fuel our professional work as leaders, and to embrace the community of a triune God.

We wonder deeply about how to live in community like the Trinity so much we have dubbed ourselves the Trinity Team. We fit together like a hexagon and have loved deeply from the start. It is a magical group where I am rediscovering me and the joy of living in authentic community. I am reminded consistently how staying in healthy connection with God, myself, others, and my earth allows me the joyous moments of reclaiming Eden, my home away from home.

As I leave the comforts of my writing closet to reveal the heart content I have carefully and painstakingly crafted, I wonder if it will be enough. Enough to be noticed, read, inspirational, even criticized, and I find myself searching wildly for Eden. The place where all is right, pain is absent, and love is the guiding force swirling around and between each of us pulling us toward Eden, where shame and fear are unknown, and the certainty we are deeply and dearly loved is the garment that covers our nakedness. Where I am always and eternally enough.

Then quietly and tenderly I hear a gentle, soft breeze whisper "I AM here" as I am held and swept up in a loving, strong embrace.

And just like that, I found Eden. I am home.

ABOUT THE AUTHOR

JENNIFER or "Dr. Jenn" is a licensed individual marriage and family therapist, a Doctor of Leadership, a Master of Social Work, and has held a teaching license from both California and Washington and a Washington school social worker certification. Growing up in Palm Springs, California, she has Southern California roots but raised her family in Tri-Cities, Washington, where the Columbia River runs through. She received her bachelor of arts in liberal studies for teaching from Azusa Pacific University in Azusa, California where she met and married Jake from Redondo Beach, California.

After teaching several years, she realized she enjoyed parent/teacher conferences more than teaching subjects, so she pursued a career in counseling. She received her master's in social work from Walla Walla University, in Walla Walla, Washington (so good they had to name it twice). In the mental health profession, she has worked in a hospital, agency, and school as a social worker/counselor. To complement her therapy work, Jennifer received her doctorate of leadership at George Fox University in Oregon. Along with counseling, she does corporate coaching for improving community and culture in work relationships and leadership development. She is also an author and an enthusiastic presenter, offering keynotes, seminars, and workshops.

Currently, she has her own private therapy practice with her husband Jake, who is also a therapist in private practice and also does presenting and corporate coaching. Through her non-profit, NuShu Sisters, Jennifer conducts leadership workshops empowering women leaders to lead effectively together with men. Jennifer also does Leadership Coaching for organizations desiring Peer Communities and churches desiring a Peer Church. Together, Drs. Jake and Jenn have developed a couples online curriculum, One Kingdom, presented keynotes, workshops, and facilitated groups. They specialize in leadership coaching for organizations and counseling for marriages, and believe healthy leadership between the genders starts in the home. Implementing a peer marriage model, Jake and Jenn raised their two children, McKenna and Dawson, and enjoy family vacations to the Oregon Coast, movie nights, eighties love songs, and boating.

When Jennifer is not working, writing, or creating, you can find her curled up with a good book with her dog Chloe, designing jewelry, composing songs on her guitar or piano, jogging, or skiing the Columbia River that runs through her town of Richland, Washington. She is a lover of life, God, people, and the earth, and relishes the beauty of the healing power of healthy relationships and developing authentic community. You can reach her at jenniferdeanhill.com.

ENDNOTES

Introduction

1   David Livermore, *Leading with Cultural Intelligence: The New Secret to Success* (New York: AMACOM, 2010), 77.

Chapter 3: God's Original Design

1   Matthew 6:10.

Chapter 4: Marriage is a Church

1   Alanna Petroff, "The Fakes Industry is Worth $461 Billion," *CNN Business News*, April 18, 2016, money.cnn.com/2016/04/18/news/economy/fake-purses-shoes-economy-counterfeit-trade/index.html.

2   Carolyn Custis James, *Half the Church: Recapturing God's Global Vision for Women*, (Grand Rapids: Zondervan, 2011), 185.

3   Revelation 19:7; 2 Corinthians 11:2; Ephesians 5:27.

4   James Hollis, "About Jung," San Diego Friends of Jung, last modified December 12, 2013, http://jungsandiego.org/about-jung.

5   Stephen Farah, "The Archetypes of the Anima and Animus," Centre of Applied Jungian Studies, February 4, 2015 https://appliedjung.com/the-archetypes-of-the-anima-and-animus/.

6   William Keepin, *Divine Duality*, (Chino Valley, AZ: Kalindi Press, 2013), 24.

Chapter 5: Becoming Peer

1   Ruth Haley Barton, *Longing for More: A Woman's Path to Transformation in Christ* (Downers Grove, IL: IVP Books, 2010), 114–115.

2   Pepper Schwartz, "Modernizing Marriages: Equality and Flexibility Make Better Husbands and Wives," *Psychology Today*, September 1, 1994.

3   Lena Lopez Bradley, "Negotiating Marital Care: Co-Creating the Connected Egalitarian Relationship" (PhD diss., Loma Linda University School of Behavioral Health, 2013), 72.

4   Brittni J. Glenwright and Darren M. Fowler, "Implications of Egalitarianism and Religiosity on Relationship Satisfaction," *Interpersona: An International Journal on Personal Relationships* 7, no. 2 (2013): 217.

5   Glenwright and Fowler, "Implications of Egalitarianism," 217.

6   Bradley, "Negotiating Marital Care," 72.

7   Bradley, "Negotiating Marital Care," xi.

8   Schwartz, "Modernizing Marriages," 4.

9   Barton, *Longing for More*, 118–119.

Chapter 6: The Impact of the Fall on Churches

1   September 27, 2016. "Woman." Podcast audio. *The Liturgists Podcast.* https://theliturgists.com/podcast.

2   Brené Brown, *The Gifts of Imperfection: Let Go of Who You Think You're Supposed to Be and Embrace Who You Are* (Center City, MN: Hazelden Publishing, 2010), 18.

3   Carolyn Custis James, *Malestorm: Manhood Swept into the Currents of a Changing World* (Grand Rapids, MI: Zondervan, 2015), 992–999, Kindle.

4   James, *Malestorm,* 999–1006, Kindle.

5   MaryKate Morse, "Gender Wars: Biology Offers Insights to the Biblical Problem," *Priscilla Papers Academic Journal* 20, no. 1 (Winter 2006): 6-7.

6   James, *Malestorm,* 2352–2353, Kindle.

7   Scot McKnight, *The Blue Parakeet: Rethinking How You Read the Bible* (Grand Rapids, MI: Zondervan, 2008), 189.

8   bell hooks, *"Understanding Patriarchy,"* (Louisville, KY: Louisville Anarchist Federation Federation), 4.

9   Carrie A. Miles, *The Redemption of Love: Rescuing Marriage and Sexuality from the Economics of a Fallen World* (Ada, MI: Brazos Press, 2006), 48.

10   William Pollack, *Real Boys: Rescuing our Sons from the Myths of Boyhood,* (New York, NY: Henry Holt and Company, 1998): 23-25.

11   William Pollack, *Real Boys* (Melbourne: Scribble Publishing, 1999), 33.

12   David Westlake, "Why Gender Equality Matters," July 22, 2010, *Restored Relationships.* https://www.restoredrelationships. org/news/2010/07/22/why-gender-equality-matters/.

13   Jaco J. Hamman, "Resistance to Women in Ministry and the Psychodynamics of Sadness," *Pastoral Psychology* 59 (December 2010): 773, https://doi.org/10.1007/s11089-010-0299-2.

14   Felicity Dale et al., *The Black Swan Effect: A Response to Gender Hierarchy in the Church* (US: Kingdom Heart Publishing, 2014), 20, 46–47.

15   Dale et al., *The Black Swan Effect,* 20, 46–47.

16   Mark Labberton, "Cultivating Church Together: How Men Can Foster Cultures Where Women Thrive," lecture, ChurchTogether Summit, November 10, 2018.

Chapter 7: Women and Church Culture

1   Cindy Jacobs, "Responding to the Patriarchal Spirit," *Charisma Magazine,* September 30, 2000, https://www.charismamag. com/site-archives/24-uncategorised/9506-responding-to-the-patriarchal-spirit.

2 Barna Group, "Meet Those Who Love Jesus, But Not the Church," *Faith & Christianity*, March 30, 2017, accessed April 16, 2018. https://www.barna.com/research/meet-love-jesus-not-church/.

3 "Five Factors Changing Women's Relationship with Church," Barna Group, June 25, 2015, https://www.barna.com/research/five-factors-changing-womens-relationship-with-churches/.

4 Adrienne Wassink, "Women in Leadership in the Vineyard." (PhD diss., Fuller Theological Seminary, 2012), 3.

5 Barton. *Longing for More,* 78.

6 Emily Louise Zimbrick-Rogers, "A Question Mark Over My Head": *Experiences of Women ETS Members at the 2014 ETS Annual Meeting* (CBE International, 2015), 4.

7 Zimbrick-Rogers, "A Question Mark...", 4.

8 "W.E.B. Du Bois." Goodreads, accessed March 20, 2020, https://www.goodreads.com/author/show/10710.W_E_B_Du_Bois.

9 Rebecca Adams, "Men and Women Prefer Egalitarian Relationships — If Workplace Policies Support Them," *HuffPost*, January 23, 2015, https://www.huffpost.com/entry/egalitarian-relationships-policies_n_6523998.

Chapter 8: Peer Churches

1 Steve Carter, (former Lead Teaching Pastor, Willow Creek Church), in discussion with the author, April 20, 2018.

2 John Davy, "Making Christian Marriages, Making Marriage Christian: Megachurch Evangelicalism and Marriage Education." (PhD diss., University of Chicago, 2014), 45.

3 "Theology of Women in Ministry," in *Church of the Nazarene Manual* 2013-2017, 186-187. https://www.whdl.org/sites/default/files/publications/EN_manual_2013-17.pdf.

4 Davy, "Making Christian Marriages," 161-163.

5 Laura Christina Macedo Piosiadlo, Rosa Maria Godoy Serpa da Fonseca, and Rafaela Gessner, "Subordination

of Gender: Reflecting on the Vulnerability to Domestic Violence Against Women," *Escola Anna Nery* 18, no. 4 (Oct./ Dec. 2014), http://www.scielo.br/scielo.php?pid=S1414-81452014000400728&script=sci_arttext&tlng=en.

6   Emma Percy, "What Clergy Do: Especially When it Looks Like Nothing," lecture, Christ Church, Oxford, September 28, 2016.

7   Nel Noddings, *Caring: A Relational Approach to Ethics and Moral Education* (Berkeley, CA: University of California Press, 2013), 59.

8   Anthony Elliott, *Contemporary Social Theory: An Introduction* (London: Routledge, 2014), 230.

9   Hosea 11:3-4; Hosea 13:8; Isaiah 66:13; Isaiah 49:15; Isaiah 42:14.

Chapter 9: Create Healthy Community

1   Gottman Sound House Model.

2   Gottman Sound Relationship Workplace.

3   William Glasser, Staying Together: A Control Theory Guide to a Lasting Marriage (New York, NY: Harper Collins, 1995,) 18.

4   Glasser, Staying Together, 25.

5   CW 12, Para 14, https://carljungdepthpsychologysite. blog/2018/04/28/carl-jung-on-visions-anthology/#. XBbn2i2ZOfU.

6   Jared Pingleton, "Marriage Counseling: Innovative Trends, Best Practices, and Clinical Challenges," *Christian Counseling Today* 22, no.2 (November 2017): 29.

7   Hunter, *To Change the World*, 28.

8   David M. Cimbora, "Clinical Training at an Explicitly Integrative Program: Rosemead School of Psychology," *Journal of Psychology and Christianity 30*, no. 2, (Summer 2011): 137-147.

9   Gottman and Silver, *The 7 Principles,* see appendix B.

10   Karen Bridbord, "Introduction to the Sound Relationship Workplace," *The Gottman Relationship Blog,* accessed December 11, 2017, https://www.gottman.com/blog/introduction-sound-relationship-workplace/.

11   Names changed to protect identity

12   Bridbord, "Introduction to the Sound. . ." see appendix B.

13   I Thessalonians 5:11.

14   Thatcher, *God, Sex, and Marriage,* 86, Kindle.

15   Gallup, "Clifton Strengths Test."

16   Crumley, "Heterarchy and the Analysis," 3.

17   Crumley, "Heterarchy and the Analysis," 3.

18   Dr. Pepper Schwartz, interview by author, Skype from University of Washington. February 7, 2018.

19   Michelle DeSwarte, Broadly Correspondent, https://www.youtube.com/watch?v=UrnmBLB-UX4.

20   The Guardian, "The village where men are banned," https://www.theguardian.com/global-development/2015/aug/16/village-where-men-are-banned-womens-rights-kenya.

21   Ervin Dyer, "In Kenya's Umoja Village, a Sisterhood Preserves the Past, Prepares the Future," Sept. 9, 2016, 8:39 AM PDT / Updated Sept. 9, 2016, 8:39 AM PDT, https://www.nbcnews.com/news/nbcblk/kenya-s-umoja-village-sisterhood-preserves-past-prepares-future-n634391.

22   The Guardian, "The village where men are banned, " https://www.theguardian.com/global-development/2015/aug/16/village-where-men-are-banned-womens-rights-kenya.

23   Michelle DeSwarte - Broadly Correspondent, https://www.youtube.com/watch?v=UrnmBLB-UX4.

Chapter 10: Create Healthy Character

1   Jo Saxton, More Than Enchanting: Breaking Through Barriers to Influence Your World, (Downers Grove, IL, InnerVarsity Press, 2016), 74.

2   "Meet Those Who Love Jesus, But Not the Church," Barna Group, March 30, 2017, accessed April 16, 2018. https://www. barna.com/research/meet-love-jesus-not-church/.

3   Meet Those. . .," Barna Group.

4   Kendra Cherry, "The Different Types of Attachment Styles," VeryWellMind, October 28, 2019.

5   "In Charts: Religion," *The Globalist.* December 24, 2019.

6   https://positivepsychology.com/classification-character-strengths-virtues/.

7   "The Character Strengths," VIA Institute on Character, 2020, https://www.viacharacter.org/Character-Strengths.

8   "The Character Strengths," VIA, 2020.

9   "The VIA Character Strengths Survey," VIA Institute on Character, 2020.

10   "The Character Strengths," VIA Institute on Character, 2020, https://www.viacharacter.org/Character-Strengths.

11   Adam Biela, "The Paradigm of Unity in Psychology," Psicologia Comunione, 2008. http://www.psy-com.org/it/congresso-2008/relatori-del-congresso/70-the-paradigm-of-unity-in-psychology.html.

12   *Oprah Winfrey Show*, Nelson Mandela, https://www.youtube.com/watch?v=wX85KLMOnQg.

13   Mandela, *Oprah Winfrey. . ..*

14   Author unknown, https://www.pinterest.com/jdeanhill/.

15   Samuel Chand, *Leadership Pain: The Classroom for Growth.* (Nashville, TN: Thomas Nelson, 2015), 3901, Kindle.

16   VIA Institute on Character, http://www.viacharacter.org/www/character-strengths/humility#.

17   Tim Burkett, "The Wisdom of Humility," *HuffPost*, June 13, 2016. https://www.huffpost.com/entry/the-wisdom-of-humility_b_10437020.

18   "2018 EPI Report," Environmental Performance Index, 2018. https://epi.envirocenter.yale.edu/2018/report/category/hlt

19   "What is Gentle Teaching," *GentleTeaching*. https://www.gentleteaching.nl/gentle/en/wat-is-en.

20   "What is Gentle. . . ," *GentleTeaching*.

21   https://www.gentleteaching.nl/gentle/en/method/ip/proces

22   John McGee, https://www.gentleteaching.nl/gentle/en/wat-is-en/youtube.

23   https://www.gentlewaysforourplanet.org.

24   Dr. Judith Orloff, "The Power of Patience: The Importance of Patience as a Coping Skill and How to Achieve it," *Psychology Today,* September 18, 2012. https://www.psychologytoday.com/us/blog/emotional-freedom/201209/the-power-patience.

25   Meilan Solly, "The True Story Behind the Harriet Tubman Movie," *SmithsonianMag,* October 30, 2019. https://www.smithsonianmag.com/smithsonian-institution/true-story-harriet-tubman-movie-180973413/.

26   Dr. Alex Lickerman, "Patience: The Power of Waiting," *Psychology Today,* February 11, 2010. https://www.psychologytoday.com/us/blog/happiness-in-world/201002/patience.

27   Christine Figgener, "What I Learnt Pulling a Straw Out of a Turtle's Nose," *Nature,* November 6, 2018. https://www.nature.com/articles/d41586-018-07287-z.

28   Pullinger, *Chasing the Dragon*, 237.

29   Jessica Murphy, "Trudeau Gives Canada First Cabinet with Equal Number of Men and Women," *The Guardian,* November 4, 2015. https://www.theguardian.com/world/2015/nov/04/canada-cabinet-gender-diversity-justin-trudeau.

30   *HeForShe, 2019.* https://www.heforshe.org/en.

31   Psalm 23 KJV.

Chapter 11: Change Strategies

1   James Davison Hunter, *To Change the World: The Irony, Tragedy, and Possibility of Christianity in the Late Modern World* (Oxford, Oxford University Press, 2010), 45.

2   Dale et al., *The Black Swan Effect*, 36-37.

3   Joseph Heath and Andrew Potter, *The Rebel Sell: How the Counterculture Became Consumer Culture* (West Sussex, UK: Capstone, 2006), 32.

4   Dahlvig and Longman "Contributors to Women's Leadership Development," 23.

5   Dahlvig and Longman "Contributors to Women's Leadership Development," 24.

6   Kathryn Heath, Jill Flynn, and Mary Davis Holt, "Women, Find Your Voice," *Harvard Business Review,* June 2014, 285-287.

7   Dale et al., *The Black Swan Effect*, 220.

Chapter 12: Collaborative Culture of Love

1   Andrew Marin, *Love Is an Orientation: Elevating the Conversation with the Gay Community*, (Downers Grove, IL: IVP Books, 2009), 163.

2   James, *Half the Church.* Carolyn Custis James, *Half the Church,* (Grand Rapids, MI: Zondervan, 2011), Kindle 2340-2341.

3   Sue Edwards, Kelley Matthews, and Henry J. Rogers, *Mixed Ministry* (Grand Rapids: Kregel Ministry, 2008), 1065–1066, Kindle.

CPSIA information can be obtained
at www.ICGtesting.com
Printed in the USA
FSHW011026231020

9 781949 021905